RAINBOW HAIR

www.lisahaganbooks.com

Copyright © Nancy Hejna 2023

ISBN: 978-1-945962-49-3

All Rights Reserved. No part of this publication may be reproduced, stored in a retrieval system, or transmitted in any form, or by any means, electronic, mechanical, photocopying, recording or otherwise without the prior permission in writing of the copyright holders, nor be otherwise circulated in any form or binding or cover other than in which it is published and without a similar condition being imposed on the subsequent publisher.

Cover design and interior layout by Simon Hartshorne

RAINBOW HAIR

*Embracing
Inter-dimensional
Motherhood*

- a memoir

NANCY HEJNA

Contents

Foreword 9
Introduction 11
Rainbow Hair 13
Impressions of New Surroundings 19

Part I The Pit 21
Sons 23
Now What? 23
Parental Leave Rant 24
Autumnal Thoughts 26
Winter Colors 27
Winter Solstice 29
Grey Zone 31
April Hawk 33
New Fish 34
Keeping Them Close 35

Part II Informed Nostalgia 41
To My Mother 43
About Will 48
Texas Journal 53
Mount Sterling Will 56
About Joey 57
Fragile 63
Daughters 65
Mother's Day 70
On the Occasion of Will's 29th Birthday 72
Michigan 76
Blindfolded 83

Part III Glimmers ... 103
THE READING ... 105
FINE TUNING ... 111
A LITTLE MAGIC ... 113
FINALLY SPRING ... 116
THE DREAM ... 117
TO CHOOSE ... 119

Part IV Unfoldment ... 121
LEAVE YOUR COAT AT THE EDGE ... 124
TIME ZONES ... 125
SAFE ... 127
THE BIG ASK ... 131
902DJO ... 136
FREE WILL IS A BITCH ... 140
& ... 143
TAKING STOCK ... 146
BREAD CRUMBS ... 154
READY ... 158
PERFECT ... 159
PLANS ... 162
ACKNOWLEDGEMENTS ... 163

Appendix ... 167
RESOURCES ... 168
WHAT PEOPLE ARE SAYING ABOUT RAINBOW HAIR ... 170
ABOUT THE AUTHOR ... 173

Dedication

For Katie, Maggie, Will, & Joey

Foreword

This beautiful new work by Nancy Hejna, 'Rainbow Hair, Embracing Inter-dimensional Motherhood,' reassures parents that healing is possible after the passing of a child. Nancy experienced the double tragedy of having her only sons, Will and Joey, pass within two years at precisely the same age. Nancy demonstrates that inter-dimensional communication is authentic and achievable through the interaction she shares with her two sons in spirit.

From the first sign that Nancy describes on the day of her second son Joey's passing, the reader is captivated. Joey's 4-year-old nephew Elliott, who has not yet learned of his uncle's transition, has an irrefutable interaction with his beloved uncle in spirit, leading to the inspiration for the book's title.

At the same time, having two beautiful boys transition in such rapid succession profoundly influences Nancy's healing journey. But the signs from her sons slowly pierce through Nancy's sadness. Her book gently traverses the autumn, winter, and 'grey zone' of her grief and finally ends with a glimmer of a spiritual awakening in spring and summer.

Soon, the signs from Will and Joey that Nancy describes are abundant, and the overlying tone of her carefully crafted work is one of hopefulness and healing. Nancy explains, "I have two very handsome, smart, funny, loving guides walking beside me to keep me moving forward whispering, 'Mom – it's ok – you've got this.'" Indeed, as Shining Light Parents, we have *all* got this.

As a Caring Listener for Helping Parents Heal, Nancy donates her time and energy to help other parents who have just started on the path to healing. Her new book is invaluable in providing evidence to parents that our children are not gone. They are still right here, and they share in everything we do. I highly recommend this beautiful work by a Shining Light Mom who is living proof that we can all move forward and heal.

-Elizabeth Boisson,
President and Co-Founder
Helping Parents Heal
www.helpingparentsheal.org

Introduction

You wouldn't believe what once
or twice I have seen I'll just
tell you this:
only if there are angels in your head will you
ever, possibly, see one
Mary Oliver, from "The World I Live in"

There are a number of books written by the bereaved, documenting a journey through the tunnel of grief and out the other side. There are even more books written about communication between living people and souls who have passed – amazing, hopeful books.

But there can never be too many. There can never be enough stunning stories about signs, about the surviving parent finding new life, new meaning, even joy, after the passing of a child. A sign for one is a sign for all. A story of hope for one is a story of hope for all. So that is why I am drawn to offer this one as another feather gently placed on the cosmic scale, tipping it ever so slightly toward the light.

My story is not a straight line. It starts in the middle, wanders back to a beginning, and then jumps around until it lands in the present. It's made up of essays and some poetry – reflections, ruminations. The first section, after the initial essay

"Rainbow Hair," is about loss deeply experienced – but I promise it's brief. This is mostly a memoir of gratitude – one I sincerely believe will leave the reader hopeful and maybe a little bit astonished, which is exactly how I feel, even after all that has happened. Because of all that has happened.

Rainbow Hair

Daughter Kate uses the phrase, "before or after all the ends," to place events in our lives, referring to the deaths of her grandparents and two younger brothers – four separate and devastating "ends" that occurred in the span of five, short years. It's a cumulative loss. Of course, the passing of grandparents who have lived overly full lives is a much different experience than losing 26-year-old brothers. They both left this world at exactly the same age – born 2 years apart and died 2 years apart at the age of 26, under very disparate circumstances. Now forever twins in the afterlife if one is to believe that sort of thing.

This compounded tragedy leads us to travel through the day cautiously. For instance, there can be a serious lack of trust in the predictability of the universe. The idea that someone could lose not one but two brothers/sons .... well anything could happen. There is no such thing as fairness. It's all chaos. Any phone call at odd hours, even a loved one delayed in transit, leads to the immediate assumption of catastrophe. Survivor brain on red alert. When will that go away? Will it ever go away?

When Will passed in 2016 from a heroin overdose, there was some sense of destiny, relief, mixed in with excruciating sadness. We had rehearsed his death. It might have happened at any time. My job after that "end" was to make sure my other three children survived, healed. I also felt compelled to let the world know Will for who he was on this earth – a brilliant, sensitive, talented soul tortured by a relentless disease. After Joey, the boy who lit up the room with his humor, enthusiasm, energy and endless ideas, died instantly in a car accident, on the morning of his sister's wedding almost exactly two years later, after I crawled out just a little bit from the bombed-out pit of grief, my job was clear and urgent. I had to find him.

The day of the wedding holds a collective, inexplicable mix of intense and hazy memories. Many people travelled on the Labor Day weekend, navigating winding, rural roads, some from far away, to honor Kate and Adam, anticipating a joyous event. They arrived with tender thoughts of support for a family who had not-so-long-ago suffered the untenable loss of an adult child. Kim, the woman who officiated, would later say as she looked out at faces of friends and family waiting for the bride to appear, seated on the lawn of the Northern Michigan flower farm venue, she had never seen, or felt, such love. Any wedding is a miracle of intricate planning, luck plus timing, and this one was no exception. Our biggest worry going into that day, however, was a slight threat of rain. The bride had a vision of her perfect wedding, and that vision came true, briefly.

After sending Joey off to run last minute errands, I spent wedding-day-morning with Kate, my other daughter and maid-of-honor, Maggie, and the bridal party at a charming Glen Arbor setting in happy preparation. Listening to the cheerful banter between young women, friends and daughters, was a privilege. However, the buoyant mood was gradually deflated by irritation, followed by concern. Joey wasn't answering his phone. He was now a little late coming back. Then really late. Worry suffused the room. He would miss some photos and the "reveal". Kate's father, Bill, called on his way to say there was awful traffic near Traverse City. There had been an accident. My stomach flipped. One of Kate's dear friend's and bridesmaid, a physician, suggested calling local hospitals – "just in case," and she did so. We were told by one hospital the accident yielded only minor injuries. Uneasy relief, but where was Joey? He was supposed to be the driver for the wedding party. He was in the wedding party! It was not like him to be so late, or to disappoint anyone, anytime let alone on this important day. We tried to smile, to carry on, to not let the concern show through in precious photos. We had to just keep going.

Bill and I received the awful call while driving to the wedding venue. Joey had been killed in the accident we heard about – the one tying up traffic and causing Bill to be late. It was a head-on collision with a pick-up truck and Joe's tiny car. The detective said he likely died instantly. The sound that erupted from me at that moment was not human, the phone thrown down with such force, both car and phone were surely damaged. The agony, anger and sadness congealed in an emotional, physical explosion! It was uncontainable – but there was no time to feel, to think, no time! We had to act. This wedding was underway! An otherworldly momentary calm took hold and, as parents of precious still-living-children, we made the difficult, but only decision to keep the news to ourselves until after the vows, Kate and Adam would have their ceremony – and then they could decide how they wanted to continue. At least we could give them that.

The few of us who now knew were numb. It was all surreal. How could this be? How could Joey be gone – just gone? In some kind of fog, with swollen eyes I hoped didn't show, dress hiked up, heels on grassy path, I remember quickly passing by all the smiling, loving faces of those near and dear, on our way to line up for the procession. I couldn't meet the eyes of my daughters, or Adam, or his two handsome, young boys all dressed up, bubbling with excitement. My over-riding thought was, their world is about to be blown apart. On this of all days. Again.

After the ceremony, but before anyone was told what had happened, Elliott, Adam's 4-year-old son, was sitting quietly and being tended by his now "official" Aunt Maggie. Wedding party and family photos were underway in the spectacular setting of the flower garden. Photos that would later be defined by before and after anyone knew. It is not in Elliott's nature to sit, let alone sit quietly, yet there he was in the lower level of the barn where the reception was soon to begin. Maggie, very worried, but still unaware of her younger brother's death, asked Elliott what he was thinking, slightly concerned about his pensiveness. "I don't know where my friend went," he answered. "Well let's go find him," Maggie offered. "What does he look like?" she asked, thinking it must be one of the many children running around outside, cousins and progeny of friends. "He doesn't have a face – and he has rainbow hair," Elliott explained, still staring off into the interior of the barn. "Are you sure? Let's go look for him," Maggie said, somewhat taken aback. "We can't. He's died." Elliott answered sadly.

Elliott was Joey's biggest fan. Joey loved Elliott.

After absorbing the shock. After sobbing. After wailing and railing at the unfairness. Kate and Adam willed themselves upright and graciously, lovingly witnessed their only wedding reception become a wake for Joey. After the devastating announcement was made, the photographer, with tears in her eyes, walked up to me and said, "I don't know what to do? How do we do this?" Caterers stood paralyzed. The DJ scrambled to adjust to the emotion of the room. Then with some sort of amazing strength, compassion, and sensitivity the entire crowd came together. The most important people in our world – everyone was hugging, crying. Holding all of it – the highest high and lowest low imaginable.

Within minutes, the predicted dreaded rain came – a downpour – the beats of raindrops on tin roof, now a welcome distraction. Parents moved closer to sit with their adult children. Some semblance of a meal I have no memory of was about to be served. The rain cleared. Smaller children went out on the grass to play in the waning, evening light. Suddenly a sound of awe traveled through the emotional crowd. Standing at the open barn doors, looking out arm-in-arm, there it was – the most spectacular rainbow! So close you could almost touch it.

Time has passed since that day. I live as a raw nerve-ending in a world I can no longer explain, launched on a fervent mission to understand energy, my own and other's. My daughters are right there with me, yearning to find their lost brothers. I feel as though I'm back in school, ravenously consuming any and all information toward the goal of connecting with my sons. There are signs of hope. There are signs indicating they approve and support us in our efforts.

Elliott received the first one.

Impressions of New Surroundings

Everything in a state of constant change, nothing still,
all perpetual movement, transfiguration of matter.

Water flows from sky through sand to lake, waves print a
unique brief edge.

Vines visibly inch, interring what's fallen there
nature compelled, taking back what belongs to her.

I look for you in the sky,
in clouds that form and softly fade, in trees so tall,
breeze in the cottonwoods.

Who's to say you're not mingled among the atoms
conscious of my search?

Or under vines I feel growing
steadily,
covering what cannot be repaired.

PART I

THE PIT

✳ ✳ ✳

*We must embrace pain,
and burn it as fuel for our journey.*
Kenji Miyazaki

There is no one way to grieve – no formula, time frame, end point. We all come to it and through it individually.

When Will passed in 2016, I made changes that allowed for time to absorb the finality of his leaving us. I had a whole summer in a new little house, out in the middle of nature, to be quiet, listen, and begin writing, mainly in response to Will's own beautiful writings that I discovered after his death. It was my therapy. When Joey passed 2 years later, I couldn't imagine any therapy, or tool that might dig me out of that pit.

The following pieces are about the immediate aftermath – the impact – and, as promised, I do not linger here. It is essential however, to move through the seasons – to start in the darkness with nowhere to go but forward – step by step.

Sons

Sometimes, I guess, you don't get to keep them.

Now What?

I am a blank slate, wiped clean by grief.

No longer sure.

Stumbling through the daily round out of habit, sheer momentum from a past life,
the one before all this.

Your memory the undercurrent of my days.

I wait for instructions, inviting the universe to write something,
about what to do,
about why it matters – to do anything at all,
ever again.

Parental Leave Rant

A thought: new mothers and fathers get "leave" at the time a baby is born. Time to adjust and bond. How much time is ideal? 3 months? 6 months? A year?

When that child dies, at age 26, how much leave is granted then? How about two sons? To adjust to the absence – for time to rearrange the bond from mother-to-son-in-body to that of mother-to-nothingness? Maybe our society wisely knows that "leave" after the death of a child should be brief, or taken in smaller bits. Without distraction or duty, a mother may be permanently pulled into the whirlpool of her own despair.

After each death, I returned to work quickly, anxious for any focus other than my own inner hell. Pick a typical response from this list:

"How do you do it?"
"How do you get out of bed at all?"
"You seem so put together."
"You're so strong."
"I couldn't do it."
"You look so good! I would just be a wreck."

PART I THE PIT

They mean well. They always mean well. And there are those who don't know what to say, so they say nothing, just stare with terrified eyes, keeping their distance as if grief were a contagious disease, or afraid of inviting catastrophe by associating with the source of such terrible luck.

But then there are those who just know. Because they've "been there." Or at least close to "there", which, let's face it, is beyond most everyone's worst nightmare and thankfully equally rare. And they come with tears, encircling arms, and listening ears. They continue to check in, even though it may be really tough to call and simply ask, "how are you doing?"

.... and accept all the wretchedness,
realizing the pain is always there,
.... will always be there,
just under the surface, the other's mistake for reality.

Autumnal Thoughts

There's a chill off the big lake,
waves crash brazenly.

Old men and old women walk the beach now
sun, skin, the warmer pleasures assigned to memory.
They come for the immensity of it, the energy,
the vista, the horizon,
peace.

Strolling alone, or with a faithful dog
pausing in reverence, in need –
sending whispered confessions to the water,
again.

Searching the clouds for dear ones.
Strange comfort secured
in knowing it will all go on,
just as it is,
without them.

Winter Colors

From an early age I've been attracted to the colors and textures of autumn into winter, never knowing a real winter as a California child. I kept the calendar pictures of the dried grasses, dead flowers, not the pastel blooms of spring. I am likely a misplaced Midwesterner, only satisfied by many ensuing years of changing seasons near Lake Michigan. How can anyone truly experience nature without distinct seasons?

In October, once my favorite month, the Midwest fields turn the hue of dried wheat, a color impossible to capture in paint with any truth. October brings with it a fervent energy, a particular light, potential, excitement. Burning shades of red, gold, rust.

Now, after all of it – after all that is lost, I look forward to the subdued browns and grays of the December pallet – stark contrasts between almost black tree bark, white snow, blue sky. This is when the landscape best aligns with inner fields. Now I wonder when, if ever, I'll embrace the brighter colors of autumn again as I walk an empty beach, feeling guilty for disturbing the sand's enigmatic patterns. Nature is perfect. People are not.

Was this strange, early preoccupation with the beauty of the remnant, the seasonal end, preserved, frozen things, a foreshadowing? Have I drawn myself to the unspeakable? Was some part of my soul hinting at this current, unending winter of grief?

Outside, pale stalks of dune grass – leafless, brittle blooms, stoic in their rise just above the snow signal a hanging on. Somewhere, buried deep, an unseen promise gives rise to hope.

Meanwhile, predictions remain grim for an early thaw, or any thaw, from within.

Winter Solstice

I cannot touch you anymore. My fingertips have permanent, remembered traces of touching you, but not the real thing now. Not the big hugs as allowed, or squeeze of a hand, kiss to the brow. Reaching up to trim the back of your neck, the part you couldn't reach. Maybe helping to straighten a tie. Pinch your foot to wake you before class, or work, or.....

Memories of holding you as little boys stir the same ache as I search through old photos, and try to remember again how you felt.

This is when it's hard. The tangible reality of loss. Double loss.

At dusk on the winter solstice, I stood between the two sturdy, young white oaks so lovingly planted by grieving friends just a few weeks before. The darkest day of a dark year. At first I had trouble remembering exactly where the "brother trees" were, as other little trees had been added nearby. I had a moment of panic that something had happened to one of the trees. It didn't look right, bark peeling, dead leaves were a different shape. Then I realized, I was standing and looking in the wrong spot. Relief palpable.

Now running my hands over the bark of each tree in search of a kind of solace – not your skin, nor the perpetual smell of boy hair, but alive and growing. Here in the exact place where childhoods unfolded along the river, down the sledding hill with views of the library, town. Two young trees planted as close together as the tree expert would allow. Standing watch. Ready to be touched.

Grey Zone

Making decisions, even the little ones, is a problem.

The questions pile up:

What do you want to watch on TV?
Which way do you want to walk today?
Where do you want to go on vacation?
What do you want to eat for dinner?

The answer to all of these is, I don't know, it's too hard to care, but the words I say are,
"I'm ok with anything, you choose." Seemingly paralyzed, the decision-making function is unavailable.
It's greyed-out, busy.

Busy absorbing the latest book about reincarnation, or signs from the other side.

Busy holding onto a wisp of a feeling, a touch, scanning the clouds for messages,
could it be?

Busy trying not to fall apart.

Thankfully the questioner is very patient, extremely kind.
He makes the coffee.

He lightens the mood and gently guides the day until I
can muster more participation,
and this he knows may take awhile.

It's not his first rodeo, as they say.

Miraculously and best of all,
he sticks around.

April Hawk

On my own this weekend. I've spent a considerable amount of time watching a pair of red- tailed hawks, nesting in the front yard of my neighbor. Just witnessed the changing of the guard – one flew in – the other out to a tree in the tangle next to the house.

She stretched, preened, pooped – off-duty hawk.

Then I looked away briefly,
caught up in thoughts about parenting ...
and she was gone.

What are her worries?

Storms? A late April freeze?

Certainly not finding food. The surroundings are full of offerings.

She is not bothered by me, or other creatures, simple.

Caring for human offspring, however, is not simple at all.

Even when they've flown far away.

New Fish

We bought fish for the fish tank today. It's always heartwarming to introduce newcomers to an undoubtedly more deluxe, spacious situation than a crowded, boring pet store aquarium. What a strange concept – creating a miniature underwater world as entertainment and assuming what a good life is for a fish! Sometimes I feel guilty, but then I think, *well, I'm a pretty good fish parent and provide a nice, healthy fish home.* In the wild, most of these little creatures would be a meal. What is this really all about – sentient beings held captive, or providing safe harbor? I'm not sure.

Other questions arise – how often in my life will I buy new fish, or a new car? How many times will I attend yoga class, celebrate Thanksgiving, hug my daughters, kiss my grand babies before I leave this earth? It's a finite number. A finite number most of us are not privy to. Oh I can guess, project, but there are no guarantees. We have learned that lesson well enough.

So we bought new fish on a hot, July day just for something to do, not knowing if we will survive more hours in our own orchestrated fish-bowl-world than the fish themselves. Not knowing if we ourselves might be part of a larger experiment.

Maybe all of it is a simple act of hope.

Keeping Them Close

What can we do to hang on to what's left? How do we find a new kind of relationship? I've read hundreds of accounts of parents who are afraid of letting go of their grief because they fear it would be the same as letting go of their kids – as if being happy is disrespectful to those who've passed.

Nothing could be further from the truth, as I understand it.

What about that which physically remains – the clothes, belongings, favorite pair of shoes, the cell phone that holds all the text conversations, maybe the very last communication? Or what about the body – ashes versus burial? Where should the ashes go? What should the headstone say? How often should one visit the gravesite?

There is no right way, or only way to approach any of this, and our children in Spirit appreciate acknowledgement, but only as far as it comforts *us* and helps *us* move to a place of peace. This is what I've come to know.

Undoubtedly every parent is intent on keeping the memory of their child as present as possible for as long as possible. For our family it has been a rather organic process, leading to a few beautiful and meaningful rituals.

Will and Joey's bodies were cremated and some of their ashes were soon thereafter released into the center of Elk Lake, a place holding very dear childhood memories for my kids, having spent many summer weeks at nearby family lake house. The boys' father, Bill, had retired and moved up to the town of Elk Lake permanently so it was the perfect place to conduct our ceremony. During each release of ashes, close family read poems and Katie and Maggie floated flowers over the spot as we rose and fell in silent reflection on the boat, rocked by the gentle wake waves, watching the flowers drift slowly away. It was a beautiful, simple ritual. I imagine by now their essence has traveled into Lake Michigan, through vast waterways, and is mingled with all the world's oceans.

Somehow their left-over ashes ended up in my closet. I had two large mason jars for each and four smaller ones set aside for my daughters. Impulsively one day months later, I decided to combine everything into one jar, justifying it by realizing I had no idea who was in which container! The jars had never been labeled! But I was a little scared too. It all felt pretty unconventional, admittedly, and slightly ridiculous. I mean I already knew by then that it's merely symbolic in the sense that Will and Joey are everywhere else energetically and not in those jars, and I'm pretty sure they were laughing at my hesitation to sift them together like mere baking ingredients ... but I still held my breath while doing it – as if lightening might strike.

Since the co-mingling episode, I've taken some of their ashes on a hiking trip to France and secretly place them under a rock cairn at the highest trail point, overlooking the Gorge of Verdon, affording them an exquisite view. We also meant to spread some ashes at the property where the beloved Michigan Hejna house used to stand next to the Galien River but waited too long. A new house has been built there and it just doesn't feel right. The next best thing was to release some right into the Galien and we did so during Will and Joey's birthday month this past year, on a freezing March day with snow and ice still covering the riverbank. A few hasty photos were taken to document the occasion as the skin on our hands and faces burned with cold – their ashes floating southward eventually to meet up with the mighty Mississippi – then the oceans once again.

Another ritual was born after Joey's passing when a group of thoughtful friends gifted two, young White Oak trees, destined to be planted in the center of the boys' childhood hometown. White Oaks thrive in wet conditions and are the perfect choice for a town known as the "Village in a Forest." These little trees were to grow right next to each other in an area called Swan Pond, a flood plain that catches the overflow from the DesPlaines River a few times a year, and becomes a pond large enough for ducks, swans, and the occasional stranded carp. I have memories of Will and Joe wading through water up past their knees with fishing nets as big as they were, scooping up the trapped fish and returning them to the river – to freedom.

The two trees now have a view of the town library along the riverbank where the boys spent many happy hours, planted near a river path where friends passing by frequently report on how they are growing. No longer residing there, I make a point of driving through town to check on the "brother trees." One appears to be a little shorter than the other, a little less leafy, but both are healthy, reaching for the sun, their slight physical differences a reflection of the boys they memorialize.

Six months after Joey passed and after the trees were planted, we decided to create an annual event to take place in March right between the boys' birthdays. This was held at the Scout Cabin – a rustic building in the woods along the river. Our first "Hejna Brother Reunion" included a dedication for the two little trees, complete with spreading some more of the boys' ashes around their roots. March is always a tenuous weather month in the Midwest and that first gathering happened on a day following a lot of rain with grey skies, and very muddy ground in Swan Pond, but faithful friends showed up in strong numbers, wearing rubber boots, umbrellas and tender hearts. Joey's best friend, Chris, brought Joey's dog Donny along. The dog was beyond excited to be with familiar faces and smells, and it was all Chris could do to keep him from covering everyone in muddy dog kisses.

Chris had generously taken Donny into his life after Joey's passing and they had become a bonded pair. In fact, during our first incredible mediumship reading, Joey specifically thanked Chris and said this new arrangement would be a good thing for both of them. Chris often comments on how caring for Donny has changed his life for the better.

After the tree dedication, the crowd gathered at the Scout Cabin for pizza, soda, reminiscing, catching up, and lots of hugs. We brought every photo of Will and Joey we could find to sift through, prompting wonderful memories. The Hejna Brother Reunion happened exactly the same way the very next March on a sunnier day, and with the joyful addition of the boys' first nephew. Then, due to circumstances beyond anyone's control, the reunion didn't happen the next year …. or the next.

We felt angst over not pulling the reunion together for a third time. Would people start forgetting about them? Would the boys be disappointed? Would we lose touch with their friends?

As a consolation, we started a blog, appropriately titled "Hejna Brothers." Populated with our photos and little stories about them, others are invited to share their own memories of Will and Joey – capturing the good times. Followers of the blog continue to grow and it turns out this virtual, ongoing reunion is working just fine.

My closet shelf still holds a partial jar of their commingled ashes, and, as the occasion calls, we will distribute them to places meaningful to them, to us – for us and our healing – with their blessing no doubt.

We're making it up as we go along just like any other family on this difficult journey – keeping them as close as we can in unique ways – navigating an imperfect situation that seems to be ever changing.

And that's okay, because we love them and they love us.

And that's all that truly matters.

PART II

INFORMED NOSTALGIA

✽ ✽ ✽

*We must sit on the rim
of the well of darkness
and fish for fallen light
with patience*
**Pablo Neruda, from
"The Sea and the Bells"**

Here's the part that goes back in time – the "how did I get here" section. Memory is a funny thing. It is never a pure observation – always viewed backward through experiences piled up after the fact. No two people remember a point in time the same exact way. No two people will experience people the same way. Our filters are uniquely skewed.

Nevertheless, it is instructive to take measure, try to examine, in my case, what created me as a mother, how that role developed with each birth, how my own filter also changed with time, with loss, alongside a slow, bumpy spiritual awakening.

To My Mother

You wrote beautiful letters to me. Your thoughts could flow on paper without interruption, relaying happy details of a life more at peace in later years. I looked forward to these as I made my home far away in the Midwest and wrote back promptly, feeling guilty for the distance between us. My appreciation for you as a whole person, not just my mother, grew along with an awareness of Dad's frequent, unfair dismissal of your thoughts and opinions – of the lifelong struggles you endured. When you died at age 71, I wrote a letter and read it at the small memorial service arranged on a boat in Monterey Bay as we gave your ashes appropriately to the sea. At the time I was angry – angry at my sister for the incessant drama – angry at my father for his belittling – but most angry at myself for abandoning you.

You knew how to take care of vegetables, treat them tenderly, washing lettuce and stacking individual leaves in paper towel. Your salad dressing is legendary, resulting in my permanent assignment as salad provider to all potluck events complete with "the dressing." You were a good cook, though you never considered yourself one – using seasonings in the exact right amount, introducing artichokes, asparagus, exotic offerings ahead of your time in some fashion, but in others right on the culinary mark in other ways. There was a killer meatloaf, spaghetti with meat sauce (my childhood favorite), some kind of magical fried chicken people raved about. Occasionally you allowed the very innovative and exciting "TV dinner," a treat saved for when my sister and I had a babysitter – Swanson's turkey with the tiny portions of cranberry sauce, whipped potatoes – the stuffing hidden under uniform slices of turkey and gravy. I can taste it all to this day.

In the high desert summers of California, where temperatures climbed into the 100's, you would wear your wet bathing suit all day after taking a swim in our above ground pool. I can still picture the suit, a black one-piece completed by a little skirt, a modest addition in the late 1960's. With those sunglasses on, you looked like a movie star – wavy black hair in stark contrast to my own long straight blond. As I've aged, my hair is now wavy with the same shape and pattern of gray. I'm told I look much like you and am glad of that.

You played a mean game of gin rummy. On days I was home sick from school, we would play rummy as I recouped, sipping Lipton noodle soup. It was lovely. You and Dad played bridge and poker with friends. I can remember as a young child hiding in the hallway on poker nights to hear the laughter and conversation. Happy memories.

Then there was the breast cancer when I was in high school, you in your late 40's. A lump found, an entire breast and lymph nodes removed, the common, extreme surgery back then. Your strength and function never fully returned, and you worried over the diagnosis, the radical mastectomy – believing the lump may have been the result of an injury from my sister throwing something in anger, hitting you at that exact spot – this confided to me much later. The whole episode with cancer just sailed past, consumed by my teen existence, I didn't really understand the gravity. One time I saw the scar. I saw the prosthesis and was repulsed. I blamed you of course, the heavy smoking, and campaigned for you to stop, sometimes even throwing cigarettes away in desperation, but you never did. You did stop drinking however, when the doctor said it would kill you.

As a teenager, I learned it was best not to talk to you about anything important from mid-afternoon onward as you wouldn't remember much of the conversation, a situation more insidious as my sister grew older, troubled, the two of you like gasoline on fire. Vodka was always hidden under the kitchen sink and the resulting irritability and conflict – rarely physical, yelling always – peppered our days. This solidified my retreat, into books, school, and friends until a time I could escape to college. I loved you. I didn't want to be you.

You lived the world through emotion and reactivity, regret and self-denial. Any discussion was fraught with an inner static and distraction so much so it seemed doubtful you were capable of listening. You loved deeply. You loved me deeply and wanted things to be different, especially with your other daughter. I believe ultimately you felt powerless, defeated by circumstance, sharing few details about your early life – a father who died when you were so young and a mother remarried to a man whose business took the family to South America for awhile. He was subsequently killed in a car accident. Dorothy, your mother, long a widow when I came along, was a strange and frail woman who passed on when I was just four. She was placed in a "facility". You had to do this as well as take care of your younger brother, Parker, a talented musician, who in all likelihood suffered from bipolar disorder. There was mention of marijuana being involved, but little detail around his early death. Reading between the lines it appears he ended his own life. All of this curtailed your plans to escape to college. I was to succeed where you failed.

You knew shorthand, could spell anything, and typed with ease. You wrote impeccably and held down jobs on and off – legal secretary, materials management at a college, office work available to a woman of your time. You were also the family scribe as my father, even though extremely intelligent, was dyslexic, and embarrassed by his poor spelling.

You and Dad were opposites in all categories, a relationship of constant bickering, my father stoic and steady to your fretting inconsistencies. He preferred the outdoors, the desert, dry heat, self-sufficiency, camping, science, and logic. You were a city girl, who enjoyed nothing more than a restaurant meal, theater, and fine things. You adored the sea and time on the beach. You adjusted and then adjusted some more as his preferences inevitably won out. I saw the calm stability in my father and aligned myself with him as much as possible, not wanting to be "weak". I owe you an apology for this – for wanting to separate myself and ultimately leave. It was not all terrible. There were many happy times with good friends and family to counter the painful ones.

With age and, hopefully, some wisdom, I realize all was not as it appeared. There existed an undercurrent of deep affection between you and Dad. He was truly lost after your passing. My younger sister, having navigated so many difficulties is a generous, sweet soul, and we marvel at just how different our perceptions, our memories of shared childhood events can possibly be.

In that final letter I wrote years ago, I claimed that your life was my cautionary tale – that you were not equipped for what was handed to you. Maybe it's true, but I also believe you were exactly the mother I needed. To escape. To understand – and to ultimately become.

Thank you, Mom,
All my love,
Nancy

About Will

Of all my children, Will was uniquely himself, different in so many ways from his siblings. I was always playing catch-up, never quite grasping the wholeness of Will in real time. There was foreshadowing early on with a slightly more difficult pregnancy and birth, a warning that this one might be a challenge. During his infancy, I was the only person who could easily comfort him. As a toddler, he could get into more mischief in five minutes than his older sisters had managed in their combined young lives! I've often declared, had the two boys been born first, we would only have two kids, not taking any more chances.

But oh my gosh was he irresistible. Will had an endearing, silly, innocent sense of humor, big blue eyes, and an impish smile that melted all our hearts. As he grew into a handsome young man, struggling with depression and a substance use disorder, we would do anything, anything, to see that smile.

He did well in school and his teachers adored him. Social, but also shy, he never wanted to be onstage or singled out. Will wasn't competitive and had zero interest in team sports, except for a desire to try soccer when he was 7. After just a few practices, he determined it wasn't for him and coaxing him out of the car once we got to the field for practices, became futile. Will was impossibly stubborn once he set his mind to something.

He was drawn to music and wanted to play an instrument, his first choice being the violin after seeing a young violinist play on a PBS special about the Suzuki method. Will was so insistent, I took him to watch a Suzuki lesson. After about 10 minutes of listening to a group of children clumsily repeating the same three notes, he whispered, "I think I want to play the drums."

At age 12, Will began guitar lessons and developed into a talented guitar player. I have delightful memories of listening to him practice a piece incessantly, witnessing the moment he finally mastered it with his expression of complete satisfaction. Listening to and playing music was Will's sanctuary, his "higher power" – the place he refueled.

Christmas was a highlight for Will as a young child, but turned depressing as he grew into adolescence, the holiday eventually reminding him of all he was not. He usually had no means to buy gifts and felt guilty receiving them, casting a cloud over the day for his siblings. In later years, we couldn't count on him being around for any holiday and we celebrated some of them with him in various rehab facilities. Gift-giving didn't exactly come easily to Will, but when it did, it was with his whole heart. I still have my "Golden Ticket" a gift certificate he created along with his own version of a brochure for a deluxe camping spot presented to me two Christmases before he passed. Sister Kate helped, but he was the creative force and the giving made him glow with happiness.

Will was close to his sisters. Being 6 years older, Kate would become a life-long advisor, a second mother to him. He clashed more with Maggie, 4 years older, the other middle child, but later developed a deep relationship with her, sheepishly seeking her fashion and hair style expertise before any social outing. Will was always comfortable talking with girls because of having older sisters. He had many girlfriends over the years and a couple of serious relationships, one of which would end tragically and be linked to his own passing.

It's not that Will and Joey didn't fight and disagree as brothers do, but they were kindred spirits. Joey knew how to push Will's buttons to the point of pure aggravation, and then be quick enough to diffuse the situation and escape just in time. They enjoyed fishing, catching unsuspecting frogs, snakes, and exploring the outdoors near the shores of Lake Michigan with Jake, our Labrador retriever. They shared the same taste in movies, comedians, books, philosophies. Will's illness pulled them apart at times, but they always found their way back. As things got worse for Will, Joey took on the role of older brother, often having to supervise and assume damage control after an unfortunate episode.

Will was a black-and-white thinker as a child, which seems to have been a set-up for disappointment. He had difficulty accepting the imperfect, and his unmasked heroes fell hard – friends, parents in a troubled marriage, a father suddenly remote. He was a sensitive child, quick to anger, and often impatient, impulsive – this impulsivity bleeding into the risk-taking adolescent, branded as the "kid who would try anything." He became preoccupied with the big questions: Why do we die? What is the point of life? Why does adulthood seem impossibly hard and sad? Combining an existential crisis mindset with a genetic disposition toward addiction was not a healthy start to his adolescence. Will's small set of friends became progressively suspect. By age 16, he was in deep trouble with drug use and stepping into a decade of struggle.

In between several stints in rehab, half-way houses, and multiple hospital stays, Will accomplished a great deal. Education is important in the Hejna family, and Will was determined to get his college degree. He hoped to make a career in healthcare as a physician's assistant and had an internship at a hospital at the time of his passing. His later writings about his volunteer experiences reveal a tender heart and desire to help others, as well as a self- awareness that was healing. Will loved working in the hospital, ironic given the amount of time he spent as an unhappy patient in many. He pieced together his college education, one step forward two steps back, four campuses, and finally a degree in psychology with honors, presented posthumously in his 26th year.

More for him than any of my other kids, my commitment to "do what I say, and say what I do," – to always be honest, consistent, and never make a false promise as a mother – seemed critical.

Will knew, no matter what happened in his life, he could depend on me. Our relationship grew complicated. I understood how the accumulating guilt and shame turned into irritation at any sign of affection or offer of help. Still, he depended on that help – that affection – and there were moments I lived for – the pure sweet heart of Will, relaxed and enjoying this world, the company of those who loved him. I held my breath, waiting for a smile.

Texas Journal

After Will passed we found his writing – a tremendous gift, much of it composed while in various treatment facilities. His words helped us to know him in a way we were unable to while he was physically here – vulnerable, reflective, painfully insightful. We would catch occasional glimpses of *this* Will, only to have him disappear – overshadowed by guilt – hidden again behind a defensive, emotional wall.

Six months before his fatal overdose, Will spent thirty days at a program called "The Ranch" in Texas, an experience marking a turning point in his thinking allowing for a level of self-acceptance and a healing sense of peace. I like to think he carried this realization with him into the next realm, expanding into his highest, best self.

The following is an unedited excerpt from a journal he kept while at The Ranch.

"You know I made an agreement with myself today, a thought came to me, it didn't really just come to me like any other thought, and it didn't feel like a thought. It was something much bigger than that. So much of my life has been spent in utter confusion, tortuous depression, and agonizing anxiety. I've been worried for as long as I can remember and at times I'm not sure what I'm worried about, but today for the first time in my whole life, and this may sound insignificant, I had an overwhelming feeling that everything was OK. No, not just that everything was OK, but that everything was going to be OK. No, that wasn't exactly it either, it was this: I decided, not decided but, like I said, I made the agreement with myself that whatever happens, whatever the future brings, whatever happens to me, whatever becomes of me, I'm OK with it. And I know that this may sound like a victim-of-circumstance sort of thing, or like I'm giving up, or like I'm denying the fact that I can control much of my destiny – it's not that – it's just that when you live the kind of life I've lived, with all the ups and downs and brushes with death, it wears you out – it really wears you out – and after a while you kind of put yourself on the outside and you look in, and you take stock of the situation, and you say to yourself, *ya know, I've been to treatment however many times and I was never really able to stick with it – I've almost died this many times and was never really all shook up about it* – and you take this outside perspective, you know, like a doctor would take and you think, 'Well he's never been able to stay clean before and he just lost his best friend (which is really what she was) and he's tried to kill himself before, and yadda yadda yadda ....' , and you look at these facts and you say ... well .... I don't know – you wise-up I guess. And you know what? I'm really scared, I'm really scared, but I just want everybody to know that I'm OK, I'm OK with it ... you know ... and maybe I can't escape from what I always figured would be my destiny, but I'm OK with it ... with everything, and it's the best feeling in the world, and I'm not mad at anybody, and ....

I have absolutely nothing but love in my heart."

On the Mt. Sterling Trail

MOUNT STERLING WILL

Rough start out of the gate.

Self-imposed cleansing poorly concealed within a family backpacking trip,
Five thousand feet to climb in two days.

Those pancakes may not stay down,
but you don't complain, guilt.

Despite forty extra pounds, you lighten with each step.

Along Big Creek, nothing but rushing water and beauty.

Away from all that pulls to the wrong side – the razor edge of decision has no purchase here.

Six thousand feet up .... and there it is!

The smile,
Clear eyes hiding nothing,
Sweet soul – amazed just to be,
At peace,
For a time.

Happily teaching us card games around a fire.

About Joey

I was dressed in my maternity finery for a formal dinner, and looking very stylish, when child number four arrived. "Maybe we should head to the hospital instead," I said urgently as we circled the venue looking for parking. One hour of labor later, an almost 10 pounds of red-haired joy arrived on earth so smoothly as if to say, "Well, here I am, and I hope I didn't trouble you too much in the process." That theme lasted for the duration of his earthly life.

From an early age, Joey was inclined to tell stories. Something would start with a basis in fact, and then the tale would just grow and grow until someone, usually me, would ask, "Joey are you telling us a story?" He would just smile.

"I got in trouble today because I'm a little too talky," he reported at the start of second grade. His teacher asked me in to discuss things. She believed Joey needed some extra help, an IEP perhaps – a lot of energy, too distracted, maybe ADHD? I considered the source, looking around at the disorganized, distracting classroom. Joey's classmates were two-thirds boys, and not just any boys, but busy, smart, and challenging boys, I knew this because they were all Joey's friends. Plus, the teacher had voluntarily taken on an exchange student who spoke only Chinese, a boy who became one of Joey's very good pals. A rightfully exhausted teacher in way over her head, I gave her my sympathies, knowing Joey was just fine, even if he was a little too talky.

Joey's mind worked in quick, entertaining, and often mysterious ways. He always had an immediate comeback. He could out-quip all of us, especially his older brother who would steam with aggravation. His cousins called him the "funny guy." For example, when he was maybe 8 years old, riding along with me as we drove down a familiar road along the railroad tracks, lined by telephone poles standing at odd angles, one this way, the other that. Looking at the poles askew, Joey asked, "So whaddaya think – beavers or lightning?"

He was non-stop motion, especially when stressed. I can see him in my mind's eye, attempting homework, me sitting and coaxing him back to the page on the table, him pacing the floor unable to sit still. He was an anxious kid – a little vocal tick, the pacing, difficulty getting to school and separating from home for a time. He covered the anxiety well with a smile, jokes, a quick mind as he grew into the handsome, 6 foot 3 inch red-head. But it would resurface with a vengeance and occasionally become debilitating. He kept his insecurities much to himself. His older sisters sometimes could dig in and try to help, but he wouldn't allow too much prying – ever. As the youngest boy, very close to his older brother and sisters, Joey found his role as peacemaker, as the fixer. We unfairly relied on his constant smile and good nature to lighten our world.

Joey had friends, lots of friends, and they adored him, looked up to him. He was kind and accepting and did not judge others. His brother's later struggles with substances were hard episodes to take, but he navigated them pragmatically, always making room for Will's redemption. Post-college, Joey travelled alone to Africa, Costa Rica, Thailand doing volunteer work, making friends wherever he went. There is a photo of him standing in a muddy field, bending down to receive an embrace from a smiling Thai villager, almost half Joey's height, grateful for his hard work on their behalf. And, on that same trip, the story of Joey mistaking a Thai family's outdoor patio gathering for an actual restaurant. He sat down at their table, making himself at home through smiles and gestures, as the family generously shared their meal. They even invited the nice, tall American back the next evening! For an anxious young man, these travels seemed perplexing to me, but Joey craved the experience of getting out of himself, away from the familiar, if only for a limited time. It was the longer commitment to a job he may not be equipped for, the relationship cutting too close, that gave him pause.

Joey was a tinkerer, could fix all of our technological devices, had a thousand interests and acted on them. He taught himself astronomy, botany, woodworking, was learning guitar and bass, always an avid fisherman, outdoorsman. And he was the helper, especially for his health-compromised dad whom he lived with in Northern Michigan more recently.

Joey was a deep thinker, as was his brother, and the two would discuss big topics endlessly. A daily reminder on his computer discovered after he passed, stated "keep doing your stupid projects – someday you'll make the world a better place." A disappointment only to himself, he seemed on the verge of figuring out just how much he had already made the world a better place.

Joey was a giver of gifts. His suitcase was always loaded with thoughtfully purchased treasures for family and friends whenever he returned from one of his travels. He loved receiving presents too and Christmas was a highlight. The first holiday after Will passed, he made the effort to appear cheerful, the old Joey, for everyone's sake, but the following year, which unknowingly would be his last Christmas, he wanted no part of it – jobless, with no money or energy to buy, or even make presents. After a lot of encouragement, he did show up and sheepishly, quietly accepted our gifts to him. In January, without anyone knowing, Joey got busy. He started constructing woodworking projects for everyone, or found creative second-hand items, which he carefully wrapped. When our family arrived in Northern Michigan to celebrate his birthday in early March, he had a surprise

Christmas celebration ready for us, complete with decorations and lights, thoroughly infused with Joey energy. The expression on his face as we opened his offerings was priceless. I received a side table with natural branches for the base, his first real woodworking project, and a rock sculpture, perfectly flat, graduated oval stones in a tower, from his vast collection. Joey crafted his nephew, Elliott, a scooter from scratch, completed by a shark helmet from Goodwill. For his dad, a hand-made shadow box with photos of Will and Joey fishing, decorated with fishing lures. Here was the best of the Joey we knew and cherished. Our hearts were full.

Whereas Will left us his words, his writing, Joey took photos, and made movies. As if the devastation of losing Will wasn't enough, Joey bore the added weight of becoming the only brother for his sisters, the only son for his parents with sad resignation. One year after Will's death, Joey loaded up his car with gear, Donny, his dog whom he seriously considered his other brother, and spent weeks on a pilgrimage, camping and hiking around the Upper Peninsula – taking pictures, and seeking closure. He took a photo around a campfire after the day's hike – a shaft of late-afternoon sunlight pouring through tall pines illuminating the scene. Donny and Joey face the camera with radiant smiles, clearly in their element, it is imbued with something close to the divine. Joey also created a stunning video of the trip – one that sustains us to this day, portraying his soul aligned with nature, exhilarated and happy.

Being Joey's earthly mother was a role summarized as a feast of exquisite joy with a side of heartbreak. Sweet, funny, loving, he was the one willing to read all the Harry Potter books with me, and accompany me to art openings, lending his energy and enthusiasm to any project. Even though we were very close, I understood his need to pull away, figure things out as he got older. The heartbreak sits in my inability to fix the fixer. I desperately wanted to understand what was going on inside of him – to take all the pain and anxiety away. Ultimately it was a puzzle he was determined to figure out for himself and I tend to believe he would have. We will never know. What I do know, however, is just how incredibly much I miss every little thing about him.

Joeyful – definition: similar to joyful, or full of joy, but better by virtue of adding an "e"; expands joy to include energy, exuberance, excitement, enthusiasm, effervescence; to be full of "Joey" is enhanced "Joy". In other words, *Joeyful* is the best feeling ever.

Fragile

All it took was one terse phone conversation this morning with an insurance agent about Joey's accident to do it. Picture a lattice of spun sugar crumbling, or house of cards, bumped. My defenses lay in a heap replaced by hurt, anger, and deep despair. The rest of day was over for me. I'm always surprised by how little it takes.

Maybe I shouldn't be.

The alternative breathing, yoga, positive imagery, energy work – useless. I've read too much, considered one hundred confusing ways to meditate, attempted to absorb all the research into energy, the afterlife, so many sources that I don't know which ones to count on. Maybe that's the problem.

When Joey was about 12 or 13, he decided to build a structure in our backyard. He spent much of the day hauling out old pieces of wood and window frames from the garage, scouring the neighborhood for useful remnants. Once he had a critical mass, he started putting it together haphazardly. I could see the structure early on, a kind of room, and that it was unlikely to hold up, but I didn't have the heart to tell him. He was beyond enthusiastic and had some vision of what this was to be! I gently suggested improvements and supported him as he hammered away. Eventually, it became clear to him that it was all folly and wouldn't hold. His plan was flawed. He was so sad. And I was sad right along with him.

Two days ago was the one year mark of the car accident – his passing. It feels like yesterday. I think really that's what this is about. My wobbly post-Joey self is just that – a wobbly structure without a foundation, easily knocked down by not-so-dormant grief, heavy, waiting to be riled by an anniversary, or phone call, or ...

Today it's my turn to be sad. Tomorrow, I start to rebuild. This time, I'm counting on Joey for help with a better plan.

Daughters

I may have been a different mother to my daughters. The boys seemed less prepared – greater needs – bigger troubles. Somehow, I felt inherently the girls would be okay – more self-sufficient, independent from the outset – and required less from me. Maybe I projected my own experience onto them – if I could do it, so could they. I've often thought Katie possibly raised herself, with clear self-direction and drive. Maggie remains a bit of a mystery, having kept so much close to her heart – for her own survival. I feel badly her brother's needs blanketed the space, leaving little room when she was quietly hurting.

As adults, we are a fiercely bonded trio. Early on, after all the loss, we had a pact that if one of us died in untimely fashion, the other two would follow immediately, ending this "earth school" drama. Now, as a tightly woven crisis-management-grief-survival team marching forward with heavy boots, we occasionally struggle on a day-to-day basis, but if you need support getting through the thick muck, we're your people.

I talk with Katie daily and always have. She talks with Maggie at least daily and always has, routinely spending time together. Maggie and I may not talk with frequency, but when we do, it's long and deep.

They are my absolute rocks. Without them, I doubt I would be here in physical form to write these words.

Katie was born belonging to the masses. The oldest of 13 grandchildren, she spent her first months being held, passed around, smiled upon by numerous aunts, uncles, great aunts, uncles, and grandparents. On her first birthday, she was given a baby doll almost as big as she was, and knew exactly what to do with it, the first of many dolls in many photos, adept at taking every opportunity to be the one to hold future, baby cousins for as long as possible.

Social is a completely inadequate descriptive word for Katie. Throughout her childhood and teens, she had multiple groups of friends and expertly navigated the role as "communication coordinator." The cell phone was invented specifically for her. I would be kept awake by late night conversations permeating our shared bedroom wall – these were promised to be over in "just one more minute." That infectiously loud laugh, however endearing, cost her. More than once the phone was confiscated.

Katie is a work-hard/play-hard human, keeping a schedule so packed, an endless energy that boggles the mind. Not surprisingly, she excelled at school, volleyball, running marathons, and keeping up with many friends. Today, Dr. Katie is a married successful, amazing child psychologist, step-mom and new mom to her own sons, balancing life with grace, humor, and some justified tears here and there.

Six years older than Will and eight older than Joey, Katie became more like a second mother especially during the rough years, often connecting emotionally with her brothers when no one else could. Maggie also has this ability, with a wisdom that is profound.

Maggie came along 16 months after Katie. They are best friends. Maggie is a psychologist with her own practice treating adults, and may tell you she doesn't know if she's very effective, but the world and her clients will pronounce otherwise. She's good. Very good.

Maggie is selective with her social life allowing for time alone to stay centered. As a child, she was the quiet one, absorbing, retreating, the writer, the artist, studious, keeping to herself, the last one to ask for help. She dabbled with dance and figure skating, settling on volleyball as a sport. High school was not fun. I think Maggie had outgrown it long before she arrived and it proved tortuous. And then Will's troubles overshadowed our lives. She was not the squeaky wheel, instead quietly working, solving her own problems to emerge as the wise, compassionate young woman with incredible self-awareness and a razor-sharp wit.

Maggie is our family's style consultant, event coordinator, perfect gift finder and giver. She calls this her 'love language' and has an artistic eye that can reorganize a shelf or transform a room into a visual masterpiece. She can arrange a table for any holiday that will take your breath away. She'll pick out an outfit you'd never consider and it will be your instant favorite. Maggie has perfected the art of shopping, online shopping, window shopping, second-hand shopping, all done mainly on behalf of those she loves. If you take the plunge and go to a Goodwill with her, bring a sandwich and prepare for a halftime nap in your car, sure to be presented with the ultimate find for your trouble.

Maggie doesn't believe she's beautiful, but she is. Both girls are undeniably stunning. Maggie was born with fuzzy copper hair, just like her new little nephew. She and Joey are redheads through and through. Katie's hair turned from blond to red in her teens, leaving Will as the only non-redhead. It's a powerful gene! To find all four Hejna kids in old photos at any age is to see a handsome group, bound together by a visible love, the air around them vibrating – treasures locked in time, our physical eyes no longer useful when searching for new images. We have to use our hearts now and that takes practice.

We are navigating a drastically altered, fragile reality. Katie and Maggie may not have required as much mothering when younger, but both have made clear they need it now. I am deeply privileged to oblige.

And I need my daughters.

More than ever.

Mother's Day

If you think about it too much, the act of putting ideas into solid form,
the written word on paper – irrevocable – no one would ever do it.

Thoughts live happily as anonymous vapor.

Words, once declared, are eternal.

The passionate letter telling of love
long since disavowed,
becomes an embarrassment.

Phrases such as there's been an accident, can sink you with their weight.

But I have a poem penned in slanted, tiny script left for me to find on Mother's Day –
his last here.

Face down on the table so that I passed it by at first,
causing worry to the author imagining,
I wasn't pleased.

The poem so rare and exquisite, that I read it again and again when the courage builds. Words from a boy who left few words.

A poet who surprised himself,
and did not think about it too much.

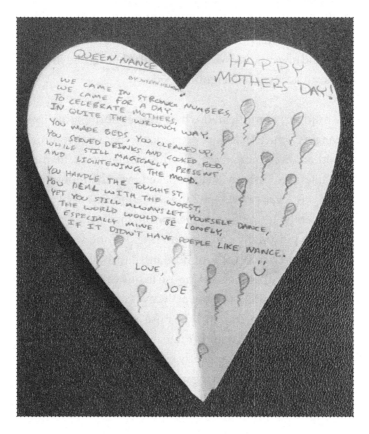

On the Occasion of Will's 29th Birthday

Will would be 29 today but has been gone now for two-and-a-half years as I write this. From a young age, he loved animals and was undeniable. As a result of Will's relentless childhood campaigns, although his siblings and father were also culpable, we had a string of pets – including, but not limited to, gerbils, hamsters, rabbits, guinea pigs, mice, ferrets (the worst phase), turtles, snakes, lizards, fish, birds, dogs, and always cats. We were a popular household in those years, an accessible, neighborhood zoo.

It would get complicated when entire food chains lived among us – mice that were pets, snakes that were routinely fed other anonymous mice, cats that wanted to eat all mice. One fateful afternoon, a cat knocked over the mouse cage leading to a massacre. One little white mouse survived but was severely injured. For some reason, I just couldn't bring myself to personally end his suffering. Frantic with a kind of misplaced panic, without thinking it through, I took the little white lump of mauled mouse to our veterinarian. All I wanted was for them to place a piece of cotton with ether, or whatever they use, over its little nose and send him off free of pain, something I couldn't muster. The young vet didn't understand at first. After gently examining the mouse, as he regarded my ceaseless crying respectfully, but with a tinge of wariness, he proposed all the things they could do medically to save the mouse, explaining, "It was unlikely the mouse would make it through because of certain internal injuries, and the interventions were somewhat gruesome." I must have looked crazed. This ridiculous litany of medical treatments was so absurd given the situation. My response was to cry even harder. I apologized for the over-reaction which, it seemed, was simply out of my control. What was all this crying about? I struggled to think, a distant foreshadowing? I certainly didn't know. I just shook my head and begged him to please, please humanely euthanize the mouse. Of all the creatures in my care to mourn that intensely! It's hard to imagine now.

There was the time a boa constrictor escaped from his basement terrarium and was never found. Never. This was not disclosed to my mother-in-law who, deathly afraid of snakes, surely would not set foot in our house again had she known. And I desperately, selfishly needed her help with four kids who were often reminded, "do not tell Grandma about the snake. Ever."

Another pet story – the world's best dog, Jake. At age 10, Will had steadfastly saved up money for Jake's small crate, part of the bargain for him getting a dog. Somewhere there exists a photo of Will sleeping on the floor next to the crate – little black ball of fur within, so small. The boys and Jake would spend long, summer afternoons exploring the banks of the Galien River, beaming, covered in mud on their return – or swimming in Lake Michigan where Jake would retrieve endless sticks. When he was about 6-months old, Jake mistook a boat on the horizon as something he needed to swim out to and retrieve. He took off paddling, ignoring our cries to come back, so far out we were sure he'd drown from exhaustion – a tiny, disappearing black dot. Will was frantic! Finally Jake turned around and made it to shore – no worse for wear – a lesson for all of us on retriever swimming stamina. Jake would be Will's companion and my security guard – patient, happy, eventually lumpy as Labs sometimes get, and leaving us at age 14. Jake left an empty space in our home and hearts which took a long time to even remotely fill.

There were so many photos of Will over the years – smiling, surprised – enraptured by the latest addition to the menagerie – box turtles, rabbits, kittens. Unfortunately, we failed at ferrets. The first one purchased from a pet store was so outright mean we were all terrified to be near it. I vividly recall cries of, "Mom help! Come get the ferret! He's running around and trying to bite me!" We returned to the store with that one and a smug assistant reluctantly handed us a more docile replacement. Of course, the smell soon overwhelmed any remaining ferret affection.

Much later, as a young man with a lasting love for animals but long past the Hejna Zoo days, Will became a voracious reader and talented writer. After he left us so suddenly at age 26, we found journals, essays, and poetry – gifts from him that are treasured. On this 29th birthday in another realm, I picture him somewhere – out there, eagerly making his way through a stack of books, pen in hand, a furry companion nearby. His brother behind him, having just arrived – pacing, pestering him to finish so they can set out on another celestial adventure. This is what my heart sees. This is what I wish.

Happy 29th Birthday, Wilbur.
I love you,
Mom

MICHIGAN

Sometime in the 1930s, my ex-husband's grandfather, the first William Hejna, made the best financial decision of his life. For very little money, he purchased property along the shores of Lake Michigan in a small harbor town called New Buffalo. At the time, most of the communities dotting the southwest coast along the Red Arrow Highway were ethnic in nature – summer get-always for Chicago's diverse neighborhoods. New Buffalo, for example, was primarily Czech, and Union Pier, just down the road, was Italian. New Buffalo has retained a little of its Czech heritage in the form of Camp Sokol, which still exists as a family camp next to the Hejna property.

Bill's grandfather, a dentist by trade with a vast social network, would host lavish barbecues at his modest New Buffalo house, many of Czech and Italian heritage. Along the way, he and his two high school aged sons built four small cottages across the road from the lake, which would become homes to extended family and close friends, first rented, then owned. Later, when his sons were grown, he asked them to pick from the remaining empty lots to build their own home. My future-father-in-law, the second William, wisely chose to locate his house on a bluff overlooking the Galien river and not on the lakefront, which would have been the more logical, lucrative choice. As a result, he combined the best of two worlds – an incredible view of the protected wetlands from the back of the house, with a quick walk across the street to the beach. This was to become the center of memorable family gatherings for years to come.

When I joined the scene around 1980, a large, screened-in porch had been added to the original rectangular house with plans for a grand, two-story addition to accommodate four married children and the inevitable grandchildren. After spending endless summers in a tiny kitchen with no ventilation cooking for large crowds, my mother-in-law, Gerry, took the opportunity to plan a huge open kitchen with two of everything and tons of storage, and it was spectacular! The kitchen island was so big we used to joke that all the exercise you'd ever need was the walking required to find an object in the thousand disorganized drawers. The large porch became a massive kitchen and dining area, with windows all along the back of the house. Bedrooms were also added and a second story master suite – room for everyone to be there at once.

The atmosphere at the big house was completely relaxed, with few rules, and, by design, the perfect weekend escape for families with little kids. My in-laws were poised to become the ultimate grandparents and for the next two decades, their offspring complied – thirteen grandchildren arrived in rapid succession, four belonging to me. Katie was the first. I remember placing her baby carrier in the middle of the dining room table with all the Hejna adults seated in rapt attention, watching her every move with delight. Each grandbaby thereafter was welcomed with the same love and devotion.

The New Buffalo house was a young mother's haven. I imagine it being similar to tribal living, where women share childcare duties, lifting the burden for all. Our collective children would run in a pack, wildlings in the Midwest jungle, the smallest kept indoors until old enough to roam. One or two of the moms would make the sacrifice and accompany the pleading throng to the beach – a Herculean task. Gerry would frequently and bravely take on beach supervision. Even though she was a non-swimming-perpetual-head-counting-grandmother, we exhausted mothers wouldn't bat an eye. Her vigilance far outweighed an obvious lack of water rescue ability in our minds. I can still hear Gerry's shouts from the water's edge with arms waving, "You're out too far! Come on back! Only up to your knees!!" At the end of the day, after a vat of chili and hot dogs were consumed, finished off by a trip to Dairy Queen, a kiddie pool on the deck would be filled with warm water and baby soap, each child splashing and laughing, while becoming marginally clean. Then they would fall asleep in a heap like puppies on scattered pillows in the big living room as nearby parents chatted quietly into the night.

"We're going to Michigan!" was possibly the happiest declaration in my children's memory. Loading up the car, including various dogs, cats, and even a rabbit over the years, was a joyful task. The ninety minutes it took to get there could not pass quickly enough, watching the scenery change from suburb to city – industry to fields of green. Upon arrival, everything just slowed down. You could breathe in the calm and anticipate the peace. It was some time before my kids realized "Michigan" was not just a house we went to but an entire State. Still, that word for our family is attached to one treasured place.

Activities changed as the grandkids grew. One summer, my father-in-law, an orthopedic surgeon and hospital administrator who loved nothing more than being a grandfather, built from scratch a huge wooden play structure. He enjoyed constructing things and was up to any challenge so, having studied several commercial playgrounds, he convinced himself he could do better. He spent hours and hours sawing and hammering, and the result was uniquely amazing. There were labyrinthine tunnels, multiple levels, a slide, swings, and more. It was enjoyed for many summers. At some point, Grandpa Hejna had an old wooden boat hauled into the yard simply for the kids to play on. It was used as a pretend pirate ship with great enthusiasm even into the grandchildren's teen years when nothing but mischief occurred below deck, including smoking cigarettes, starting a fire in the hold, and other shenanigans. The ship lost its appeal as it began to rot, and transformed into a home for feral cats and wild bees.

The love of fishing is a strong genetic trait attached to the "Y" chromosome in the extended family, and my boys were no exception. Following their dad's and grandfather's examples, Will and Joey would disappear for hours fishing the Galien, either on foot or row boat, and jump at any chance to go out on the big lake. There were also summers full of kayaking (my personal favorite), skimboards (handmade by the grandpa), a little water skiing, and plenty of swimming. The cousins learned to golf in Michigan, how to build a proper bonfire, how to set off fireworks on the Fourth of July without losing fingers, or igniting nearby homes, (*not* my personal favorite).

My parents drove their RV all the way from California to stay in New Buffalo for a couple of summer weeks. Having agreed it was too arduous to travel during the holidays, this was our annual reunion, however, one Thanksgiving, they decided to risk the Midwest weather and spend it with us in Michigan. My father-in-law was a stickler for everyone being around the same table for holiday meals. Still, there wasn't one large enough to accommodate almost 30 people that particular Thanksgiving, so they built one – on the spot! A table top so huge it required two large round antique tables at each end to support it as a base. Passersby looking for Camp Sokol next door, would see the massive table and large kitchen through the window and assume it must be the dining hall for the camp.

Even post-divorce, my relationship with the Hejna family and the Michigan house remained virtually the same. They continued to treat me as a daughter, and I continued to bring the kids out most summer weekends. I'm convinced this arrangement may have saved my sanity. Vacations with four kids are daunting and expensive. Time spent at the Michigan house was an incredible blessing. Once a summer, I reserved a weekend to host a gathering for my friends – the people who took care of me throughout the year. As a single parent, I was dependent upon generous invitations to holiday parties and other events. At its peak, upwards of 60 people would show up. Everyone looked forward to the annual open house, complete with an enormous potluck dinner on the deck, then stuffing as many families as possible into beds or sleeping bags at the end of a day on the beach.

Michigan shaped our lives. My children grew up with close ties to cousins, aunts, uncles, and grandparents that continue. They learned to appreciate the wildness of the river and wetlands and respect the changeable waters of the lake. In fact, Will's first brush with death came at age nine during one of my gatherings. The waves were big that day which made for very exhilarating swimming, but also the potential for rip currents. Kids were chastened to stay near the shore with their feet on the bottom. Will was not that far out but drifted to where he was over his head, and the current was holding him there – pushing him slowly away from land. It was one of the dads who first noticed his struggle and, without hesitation, dove in, swimming quickly out to scoop up a very tired and scared Will. Another minute and he would have gone under, too exhausted to fight the current. Thinking about it still gives me chills.

The cousins are adults now – some with babies of their own – all with busy lives. When the grandparents left this earth, hard decisions had to be made about what to do with the Michigan house. It became progressively in worse shape, and no one had time to take care of it – certainly not in the way it had been. Eventually, the property was sold and the house torn down – one more loss on the tally sheet of losses.

But the memories remain vivid and timeless. Even now, many years later, the view from the Michigan house is etched in my mind, leaning over the deck railing, gazing for hours at vast wetlands – hint of the river, dotted with oak trees, accompanied by a thousand bird chorus.

It's still my favorite place in all the world.

Blindfolded

YMCA CAMP 1966-1969:
It may have all started blindfolded on a hill called "Ragger's Mountain" at Camp Earl Anna, a YMCA camp which still exists somewhere near the Mojave Desert. This was part of a ceremony whereby a camper, in this case 10-year-old-me, was led to the top of a hill in silence, a bandana around their eyes adding to the mystery, and left to sit and consider a spiritual pledge for the coming year. The first would have been at the "blue" level – a beginning "ragger." Blue level was fairly general – promising to be kind, to think about God in the-big-picture sense, to do "good things." I remember even now, 54 years later, the exact feeling of sitting blindfolded, fragrance of heat on pine, listening to breezes whispering through trees, and coming to realize something was "out there," something much bigger than me. I wanted to be part of it.

I made a secret pledge to myself, the blue rag was tied around my neck proudly, a large square of fabric with a YMCA logo printed on it. Later that week we boarded the bus back to Burbank where we were collected by our respective parents, but I felt changed somehow. A door had been opened, just a crack, even though my blue rag ended up in a drawer until the following summer. I would return to Camp Earl Anna and repeat the ceremony twice more, committing to a brown and silver rag. Then turning 13, I was no longer of age.

During those formative years, I lived for the one week each summer away at YMCA camp. I worshipped the counselors, loved the campfires, the fellowship, the songs. I have come to appreciate the YMCA's open approach to spirituality, their focus on developing good character, and realize, looking back, that my camp experiences created the foundation for a lifetime of searching for all that is "bigger."

CHURCH HOPPING, 1969-1974:

We moved a lot before I turned 8, but my mother always found some denomination of Protestant church to attend wherever we might be living. I hazily recall a Methodist Church and their annual Christmas craft bazaar where I fell in love with a handmade, stuffed frog gratefully purchased for me. Memories are scant.

The Presbyterian Church of my middle school years in Newhall yields fond memories of youth group trips led by a dad who was a Sunday school teacher and wore comically short pants.

I remember the joy of singing in a choir and being good friends with the daughter of the minister. Presbyterians do not make a habit of serving communion, but do so on occasion. Having an inside connection, after the service on communion Sundays, Kim, the minister's daughter, and I would grab all the left over always delicious, chewy-kind of bread, and grape juice, race to the girl's bathroom in back of the church and eat as much as we could while locked in the stalls with no attention paid to the fact that we were technically ingesting a lot of Christ's "body and blood" all at one time. Kim had an annoying older brother who would attempt to take it from us, but wouldn't dare venture into the girl's bathroom.

In high school I decided to do some church-sampling. At this point, my spiritual framework might have been summarized as follows: I believe there is something bigger than me; I believe we have a purpose; I know there are a lot of different ways to look at this, but I haven't found any one way that feels right to date. The search continues.

Catholicism seemed much too intimidating and confusing. After attending some run-of-the mill Protestant churches with little satisfaction, I felt the need to branch out. It just so happened a friend who was a Mormon (there was a significant population of LDS in our small, Southern California farm town) invited me to a Sunday School class of sorts. What I recall most about the day was being extremely uncomfortable as the teacher came up to where I was sitting, while relaying a biblical story having to do with 'many-strands-making-one-strong-rope.' Standing behind me, he reached out without warning and lifted my hair, which was in a long, thick ponytail, up to the class as an example!

I was mortified. For this and other theoretical reasons, Mormonism was crossed off my list.

Another friend, Kathy, was what my parent's called a "holy roller." This was intriguing. I attended services with her one Sunday as a member of a guitar group of four girls, of which Kathy and I were half. I thus experienced the Assembly of God congregation in full-force. (Let us first imagine listening to four adolescent girls each with a guitar, none possibly in tune, sing folk songs with "harmony." Turns out, our respective churches were our only bookings.) Besides our performance, there was a lot going on that morning in Kathy's church – no comparison to Presbyterians, none. I witnessed speaking in tongues (which was eerily fascinating), spontaneous public confession and being "saved," even a possible hands-on-healing. I'm not sure. I was in a state of shock. It was all entertaining and much too strange to absorb.

My hasty conclusion after sampling, granted in a limited way, a number of faiths, was that organized religion seriously lacked what I craved – spirituality. I came away with little reverence for all the rules, ceremony, judgement, and inevitable exclusion. It would be years before I again participated in any kind of formal religious activity, and only then in an effort to introduce my own children to "religion" so they'd have something to rebel against.

THE AGNOSTIC COLLEGE YEARS, 1974-1978:

At age 20, I found the book *Illusions* by Richard Bach, of Jonathan Livingston Seagull fame, and was riveted! To this day, my original worn-to-the-point-of-falling-apart-with-notes-and-highlights, original little paperback copy sits on the bed-stand. I tucked the radical message of *Illusions* – that we are all our own messiah, that we are all part of God – into the back of my mind to be unpacked later. A world religion class my freshman year, a decent introduction to Eastern religions and philosophies, was helpful. I was intrigued by Buddhism and would later in life spend time "sitting" in front of a white wall with open eyes for weekly meditation, and listen to Dharma talks at a Zen Buddhist center in Chicago. Most of the "congregation" was composed of psychologists looking for peace of mind in the midst of their intense work-a-day.

MYSTICAL DETOUR, 1985-1987:

As a new mother with few friends in a new town, I did a lot of reading. Still searching for the meaning of it all, I read far and wide and into the weeds. Shirley MacLaine published books about her out-of-body experiences and contacts with extra-terrestrials that I found absolutely fascinating. She bravely withstood a lot of criticism as a result. I traversed through many New Age-y philosophies, picking up pieces of information that seemed to intuitively fit, but didn't talk to anyone about any of it. My family and community felt much too conservative. I tempered my curiosity and enthusiasm for such "out there" theories. It was enough I was bordering on vegetarianism and came from California. This would not fly.

PRESBYTERIAN – AGAIN, 1990-2000:

When my oldest children, both lovely, mostly compliant little girls, were in elementary school, it felt right to become involved as a family in "church." We lived in a church-y community. The minister of the Presbyterian church was a friend to my in-laws, had pronounced my husband and I married (without using the word "God" too much, per my request) – it felt comfortable. The congregation appeared to be an open-minded, accepting group. So I jumped in – with both feet, as a matter of fact. I ended up volunteering to the point where the grimy, little petty things and how a church is really run by imperfect humans becomes known, which can be deflating. Any mystery and loveliness ended up tarnished. Along the way, however, I met some wonderful people who helped others with no strings attached and was part of a certain Christian momentum for a while. I was even baptized by the youth minister, who explained she was placing the "mark of God" on my forehead. I liked that explanation. It had nothing to do with salvation. I liked that I had a way for God to find me more easily. Much later in life, as it turns out, this very spot on my forehead, corresponding to what many call "the third eye," has become quite sensitive to "energy." My children – two who were baptized when they were old enough to make the decision for themselves (the aforementioned compliant girls), and the other two not-so-compliant-non-baptized younger boys, were given enough of a foundation to make up their own minds. And they have.

GRIEF AND A MELT DOWN, 1994:

When I was 38, my mother died. We had that complicated relationship, but I loved her and felt very protective of her. This was my first significant encounter with death and I was derailed, broken open in a way that shattered my whole self-image. In the days soon after, I became aware of synchronicities I could not explain. I heard a voice in my head clearly that told me I needed to start painting, making art, a passion long put aside, and it was not my voice. My dead mother came to me, so alive so vibrant, in a dream and told me she was fine and gave me some instructions. I would later learn this was a dream visit. I went from confused, deep grief into a mid-life crisis and spiritual awakening (partial), all of which did not bode well for a marriage already skating on pretty thin ice. This thing happening to me understandably scared my husband. It scared me too. The marriage survived, barely and not well, for another few years. Life took on new meaning, new direction along with a lot of heart-ache. Bottom line – it's advisable to figure out who you really are, spiritually and otherwise, before getting married, having four children, and becoming immersed in a small, conservative community in which divorce seemed extremely rare.

CRASH COURSE, 2018-PRESENT:
Even after an intense "mystical" experience, the day-to-day grind, with all its minutiae, takes over. The glow of a new "knowing" fades in the face of boots-on-the-ground concerns. For many years after my mother's death, I operated in mostly happy survival mode, raising four kids, working, trying to create. Layered on top were Will's eventual bouts with deepening anxiety, depression, drug dependency, and all that brings with it for a family. Then his death – not unexpected after years of near misses. Will's passing was not the catalyst and I find that interesting. I did not drop everything to look for him, or find meaning. As mentioned earlier, there was a sense of inevitability, a peacefulness finally granted to Will – and, if I'm honest, also to us. No, it was Joey's sudden, absolutely unexpected passing that launched me like a rocket into next-level spiritual school. And I realize, looking back, that all of the moments of intuitive awe, all of the little pieces of spiritual wisdom gathered through the years, starting with listening closely to that something-bigger-than-me while blindfolded on Ragger's Mountain, have led to this moment. I have been prepared, bit by bit, to unfold into the "knowing" that we continue on after death – that my sons continue to exist in a different

way – that my boys are teaching me how to navigate my new role as an inter-dimensional mother. It has not been a straight path, but there is a path. I do not walk it alone, nor have I ever, but now I have two very handsome, smart, funny, loving guides walking beside me to keep me moving forward whispering, "Mom – it's ok – you've got this."

With my cute, silly boys – Happy days

The boys with their dad, Bill

Joey & Elliott

Will's elusive smile — Elk Lake, Michiga

All smiles – Communal bath time

*Maggie and the boys – Christmas in Arizona
- hiking Camelback Mountain*

Katie, Maggie, Joey, Will – Joey's college graduation weekend Bloomington, Indiana

Katie and the boys – Wisconsin winter getaway

Joey on a volunteer trip with a grateful Thai villager

*Joey and his dog, Donny – camping
Porcupine Mountains, Michigan*

Brothers

Christmas sweaters and a few missing teeth

PART III

GLIMMERS

✼ ✼ ✼

....

The world is full of magic things,
patiently waiting for our senses to grow sharper.
W.B. Yeats

....

I'm really not sure where my daughters and I would be without our first evidential mediumship reading. Maybe something similar would have happened. Maybe we would have muddled along for another year or two – desperate and searching. Maybe we would remain in a very dark place.

The magic began in a Chicago hotel conference room, of all places, and continues to this day. In the beginning – hopeful slivers of light hinting at a much bigger reality. Enjoy the glimmers.

The Reading

It was Thanksgiving dinner in Northern Michigan, just shy of 3 months after Joey's passing, 2 years after Will's. There seemed to be an unspoken collective need to be together whenever possible, aunts, uncles, and cousins. I was reluctant to bring it up, and urged my daughters to open the subject with their aunt, my sister-in-law, the only person we knew who had seen a "medium." Our curiosity was palpable. The three of us, daughters Katie and Maggie and I, had a pending in-person appointment with a medium in early December. We were united in our desire to communicate with the boys. Was it possible? We figured we had nothing to lose. Kate researched and found the best, most recommended, and not inexpensive I might add, medium in the area. We were anxious to know what to expect, trying to keep our hopes in check. My sister-in-law was thankfully happy to share her experience, which seemed incredible to us and also encouraging. During her own reading, she was confident her mother came through with clear messages. The session had given her immense peace and assurance that her mom was still very present in her life.

The day came for our family reading with the chosen medium. We arrived at a fancy Chicago hotel – minds swirling, nerves buzzing. The medium, so well-spoken and professional in appearance, greeted us warmly and her lovely Midwest persona eased our anxiety almost immediately. We sat in a formal conference room at the end of a large table. It felt "corporate" and strange, incongruent to the task at hand. She began by explaining her history, how she worked and connected with "spirit," the importance of an "evidential reading," and then jumped into the session with our three cell phones lined up and set to record. She explained there would likely be information that may not make immediate sense, but would be important later. We would need time to reflect and digest all the details. Over the next hour, by virtue of what took place in that conference room, our world view encountered a seismic shift. A different sense of "reality" seemed not only possible, but virtually undeniable. We were given a life-line. We were given hope.

To begin, the medium moved her attention inward very quickly. She described the process as opening a gate, tuning to a frequency as one would a radio dial. Almost immediately my father came through! The medium captured his personality, appearance, and circumstances of his life and death precisely. I was so touched and amazed! My dad mentioned I should "call my only sister more," a phrase he had used many times, always his hope that we would be closer as sisters. Then he faded into the background and made way for other spirit visitors from his generation to make their presence known – my mother-in-law, mother, a quick hello from my father-in-law, all with accurate evidence – then the moment we had been waiting, hoping, for: "I have a young man here. He gives me the impression that he is a son," she said. It was Will! He was with us in the room! Once again, the medium accurately described him, his passing, his appearance and personality – details that were known only to us. An example – Will relayed that he was very proud of a diploma he had worked incredibly hard to earn – all true. He also knew Katie, Maggie, and I had been the ones to receive his college diploma after his passing as he had been present in spirit for the brief ceremony. He referred to the piece of paper, his diploma, as "gold." He also described the memory of how I frequently bought expensive protein powder for him when he was in his working-out/muscle-building phases because he couldn't afford it. Quirky details that could only come from him. Validations.

Then Joey stepped forward. At first, the medium was confused by a personality shift and continued sense of a "son" presence. When we explained two sons/brothers were in spirit, she paused to share her deep condolence for our double loss, "lightning striking twice" as she stated. She soon sorted their different personalities out rather easily. Joey had a lot to convey – an apology for his aloofness and emotional struggles before he passed that "were not himself." Assurance that he was happy now, together with Will, and very busy. They joked around, clearly their same earthly personalities coming through. There was Joey's concern over the whereabouts of his passport, an object quite significant to him with the record of many volunteer trips and travels. At the time, I thought we knew where it was, but promised to track it down. His description during the session of where to find it was a tremendous piece of evidence, a story that evolved long after the reading was over. Without his guidance, Joey's passport would have certainly been lost to us, given away in a box of random items set aside for the Goodwill. Both Will and Joey were excited for us to know they were continuing pursuits important to them in this life. For Will that was study, reading and writing. For Joey, he was traveling the world – all the places he was unable to see in his short life here. Together, they were helping others on earth, even beyond family. Both wanted us to know they were present in our lives and gave us the signs we should pay attention to. We had already picked up on a few. Katie found rainbows in multiple forms everywhere. Maggie seemed to have electronics, especially her computer, act strangely. I had lights flickering, birds appearing. At one point during the reading, Will brought attention to the top of his head, touching it several times. According to the medium, Joey similarly touched his forehead. It would take me a few more readings, with a few more excellent mediums to realize Will and Joey were trying to indicate where I would feel their energy coming in. They call this clairsentience and it turns out to be my strongest "extra" sense. I can feel their energy in exactly those places, Will on top of my head, and Joey in the middle of my forehead – usually when they are trying to get my attention, often leading to other signs, such as a song playing with a perfect message, also when I'm thinking about them, or talking to them.

One of the most evidential exchanges had to do with three bracelets that were supposed to be identical and made by an artist in their honor. The boys said these were to be "nice and not cheap plastic." We should have them designed and made. Will and Joey came back with details about the bracelets twice during the session and emphasized their importance. We didn't understand the reference, but agreed it would be wonderful to have such a thing. It so happened, at the time of the reading in early December, an artist friend of ours was creating three beautiful, identical crystal bracelets as Christmas gifts to honor Will and Joey. When I opened the box in early January and saw the bracelets, linked together in three perfect circles, I knew without a doubt this was the boys' way of giving us clear evidence of their continued existence and involvement. We had no knowledge of the bracelets being made. The medium had no way of knowing. Will and Joey saw it all and relayed it to her so that we would have a piece of information that was irrefutable – a "third party validation."

We spent some extra time at the end of our session as the good-hearted medium helped us begin to absorb what just occurred, knowing how shocking and also healing a first reading can be. We walked away in a daze. Did that really just happen? Were the boys actually there? Yes, we agreed. There was no other explanation. None.

This was the turning point, the moment that allowed us to stand upright and begin to move forward through the grief, with the grief and into the ultimate reality that we don't truly die. Certainly, we've had our doubts since then, but the mountain of evidence accruing on the side of life continuing after physical death, of those who we love being very much with us, and the belief that there is indeed a future to be had together someday in some other beautiful place, is huge. And it continues to grow every day.

The bracelets foretold in The Reading

Fine Tuning

Earth-bound motherhood demands subjugation of self – stifling any interfering self-centered thoughts, emotions, and feelings in order to concentrate on the little one's needs.

Earth mother's ears are trained to a baby's breathing, the cough, the cry.

Her eyes laser focused on the climbing toddler.

With a voice that can soothe the anxious, pacing adolescent frustrated by math homework.

And a body capable of enduring an eight-hour drive to pick up a sick child, and the sleepless, fevered nights thereafter.

In later years, she counts shoes by the front door to see who's missing, then lies awake, worried until the door opens again at 2:00am.

All of this critical, earth-mothering information comes from outside sources.

Inter-dimensional motherhood requires
different abilities.

It is essential this mother become familiar with untapped
senses – internal and elusive. This develops alongside
the inevitable grief which presses down, doubles down –
hindering all efforts to rise above.

However, the reward for traveling within, trudging up
and over the steep sadness mountain – digging into
all the feelings denied, or avoided – is extraordinary
possibility,
and wonderment.

Ears buzzing, tuned inward hear a voice familiar yet?

New eyes behind the closed ones witness a meeting in
the shadows.

Electric skin detects a brushing of invisible fingers, a
slight pressure, warmth where it doesn't belong.

The inter-dimensional mother's heart becomes
cautiously hopeful – poised to discover more truth, than
she can possibly fathom.

A Little Magic

My Joey continues to have a quick, sometimes maddening sense of humor. He was a storyteller, mixing fact and fiction from an early age, and as a teenager, he could always get me going – the pretend phone call from a police station that would start with, "Mom, you're not going to like this," followed by some detailed, fake account. And just when my heart and head began to implode would come the inevitable: "I'm just kidding." I couldn't be angry for long. He was too sweet. He was too "Joey" for anyone to be upset with him for more than a minute. He was also the peacemaker within our family and between his many friends. Countless testimonials of how he smoothed over disagreements, accepted people without judgment, was friend to everyone and anyone, came to light after his passing.

At age 9, Joey encountered a rough psychological patch – some separation anxiety – trouble going to school, and intense worry when I would be away even for a little bit. The two of us saw a social worker to help him through. We only needed a few sessions, but at one point when just the counselor and myself were in the room, she said, "I envy you. He will always be close to you. Always." And it was true. He was my guy. He is my guy. We have a particular bond.

About 6 months after his passing, as signs from him were becoming apparent, I began my usual walk through the sand dunes, perpetually trying to clear my head, experience the surroundings – to listen, look at nature, and make space for energy to come in rather than think. On this particular day, I was preoccupied, consumed by loss and rather irritable. At the top of the dune, overlooking Lake Michigan, I stopped and gave myself a good talking-to about "emptying my mind." Then I just waited. After a few minutes, I heard as a thought, or a voice: "Look for a little magic." This phrase came through clearly. I hadn't experienced anything quite like it before. I began to follow the trail again, mindfully, quietly out to the shoreline. Turning to walk along the water, I was drawn to a piece of driftwood, all by itself on the vast beach, right in my path. I picked it up and was immediately delighted! In my hand was the perfect image, on all sides of the wood, mind you, of a dolphin head – carved by nature and quite detailed! My mood immediately lifted as I said "thank you" for the extraordinary sign. Upon arriving home, the driftwood dolphin was placed next to a photo of my boys, among other findings, feathers, rocks and such, I sensed were treasures from them.

Then it hit me! It had taken a moment to remember, but wow!! Not only was the piece of driftwood in the perfect shape of a dolphin a remarkable find in and of itself, but the incredible synchronicity was that Joey's friends had donated to the local zoo, adopting an animal in his honor. The animal they adopted? You guessed it – a dolphin whose name was Magic. I had been led to find a "little Magic."

I have no doubt this was a gift from the tall, sensitive, loving, red-headed boy full of mischief, now in another realm, helping to ease my pain and make things feel better, just as he always has. Still my guy. Still making me smile. Still as close as he can be.

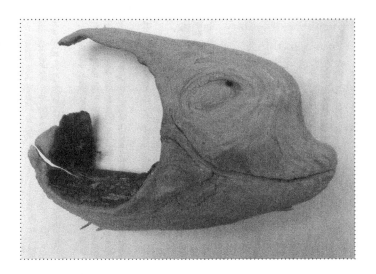

A little Magic

Finally Spring

Watching the hawk
watching me
watching the world unfurl green.

Geese, deer, clouds, in pairs, gently drawn together by
the season of extravagant flaunting.

Flash of blue, yellow, red foreshadow ritual,
the feathers temporary, fleeting,
but not everything.

Time, you see, is a trick easily played unless ....
A death gives birth to
awareness, mysteries revealed, yet how to
reconcile with only half an earthbound heart, to
be in this world, but not of it –
not anymore.

Meanwhile the bright, feathered messenger swoops so
near, signals – just for me,
and I
am
breathless.

The Dream

In the dream you appear,
quite alive
the explanation makes perfect sense.

I study you with reverence, awe
radiant is the word.

I ask – what have you been up to?

Various odds and ends, jobs, traveling, learning, but you've missed this place.

Bursting with questions, something holds me back,
the moment fragile.

Three of us now stand together
as your brother suddenly appears next to me also
not dead
in my dream so close
I can feel the joy rising.

We turn to see the beloved little boy waving, smiling.

He's the perfect blend of both of you, isn't he?

Yes – he is, we agree with full, connected hearts
as my eyes
open
to the weight of morning.

To Choose

I choose –

to listen for the wisdom of birds

to watch cloud portraits emerge, shift

to swell with the beauty of branches black against silver

to pull on a hope thread

to gaze upon lake waves and imagine you swimming

to grasp at fading dream whispers

to follow silent nudges betraying a presence

to know we are more

to know we are more

PART IV

UNFOLDMENT

✱ ✱ ✱

*Where there is great love,
there are always miracles.*
Willa Cather

I admit that I worry about my earthbound children and grandchildren. When they get in the car to drive long distances, I fret, pray, implore all the angels, spirit relatives and guides to keep them safe, because I am really, really done with the big losses.

And I'm still getting used to this new motherhood – bridging dimensions. I miss my son's physical presence, their voices, their hugs with every bone in my body. I cannot tell you I don't cry a little on most days. But more often than not, I'm very much aware that they are right here – closer to me than before – closer to their sisters, their nephew, their dad, their cousins, their friends than they ever were. And free, truly free of all the human suffering – especially Will.

I talk to my boys all the time. When one medium suggested our kids in spirit will communicate with the same frequency they did when here on earth, I thought, oh well, I'm doomed, but Will and Joey are masterful communicators in spirit. I expect them to hold up their end of this bargain we've supposedly agreed to play-out and they haven't disappointed me in any way. I continue to look into various forms of interacting, and I'm encouraged at every turn.

My level of gratitude, awe, and love for all four of my Hejna babies, across all dimensions has grown a million-fold.

PART IV UNFOLDMENT

The following writings are a few of the grander communications and realizations, pointing directly to the fact – the fact – that our relationships continue beyond physical death. Love never dies.

Leave Your Coat at the Edge

Leave your coat at the edge and come on in,
go ahead, step through.

It's neither warm nor cold where you're headed.

Pay attention!

Look for a little magic,
or light.

Just listen.

Effortlessly, there's
a thought, a voice
trust it –
why not?

Maybe ask the question,
the right question, what if?

It's ok to smile, you know,
to glow green with an open heart.

Really,
it is.

Time Zones

We humans are organized in such a cumbersome way, for example – time zones – Eastern, Central, Mountain, Pacific, etc. I just missed something I was really looking forward to, because I confused the time zone. However, my boys remembered. We had a date for this online group meditation to connect with our children in Spirit, and they gave me signs they were here – ready! I blithely continued to watch another, albeit important, video, thinking that I still had a good 45 minutes before the Zoom online meditation event. Yes, my light flickered, a sure sign from my boys, at the appointed hour in the human realm. Then it dawned on me that the meeting was posted in "Eastern Time." I had missed it.

How can two vibrational beings keep track of these things better than me with dozens of digital clocks blinking? There is no "time" as we know it, so we are told, for them!

I'm coming to learn that the heart has its own clock powered by love, and triggered by thought of connection. Conscious desire to touch across dimensions is more powerful than a Google calendar, and more accurate than the satellite-driven time piece that sits on the wrist. Appointments are kept, honored through the bond between souls.

And this cannot be broken.

Next time I'll pay closer attention to the human details. That's a promise. Will and Joey, thank you for being there, for being here – always.

Safe

In both cases, after the boys passed, we quickly sorted through their belongings and changed the appearance of their respective bedrooms. For us, it was too sad to keep things the same, but I know this isn't true for all families. Besides, neither of them had accumulated much in their young adult lives and it was a quick business to decide who should keep what, putting a few things in boxes for future consideration. Now it makes me smile to see Adam, my son-in-law, wearing one of the boys' button down shirts, or some of Joey's many pairs of shoes. Joey liked shoes.

Will's guitar now belongs to his very talented, guitar-playing cousin. Will's books line my shelves and his precious writing is carefully stored in my closet. Maybe someday, one of Will's nephews will fall in love with his navy wool coat and scarf – the one he wore so elegantly. I believe Will knew just how handsome he looked in it too.

There was one particular item belonging to Joey that I was unhappy to find and resented the task of having to deal with it. Joey had purchased a handgun, very much against my principles, and he knew it. No one was aware he had the gun until we found the small, locked case in his closet, having acquired it just before his accident. He had it licensed, and it appeared he intended to take classes to learn how to use it properly, per the paperwork found next to the locked case, even though the key was nowhere to be found. I decided to take the case to our local police station and have the gun destroyed. The following week, in a bit of a furry, I drove the case to the station, but they were closed for the day. I would have to wait until passing through town again.

The boys made it clear in our first mediumship reading their belongings should be enjoyed by others and highlighted what was important – a small woven bracelet of Joey's, for example, should be worn by his sister Maggie. The new, brown leather work boots were to go to Adam. A painting I created for Joey's most recent birthday, representing his epic camping adventure in the Upper Peninsula, needed to be returned to my house. Will's college diploma should be treasured always, and Joey's passport enshrined – both representing significant accomplishments in their lives. Joey spent considerable energy in the reading conveying where to find his passport. The medium pictured a small drawer, or box and relayed this to us. At the time, I thought I already had Joey's passport safely stored, so didn't take this too much to heart. Joey was also intent on us finding a set of keys. Again, we were pretty sure we had his keys and let these bits of questionable information float by.

Well, sure enough, I couldn't find Joey's passport or the keys. They weren't where I thought they were. I checked with Bill, the boys' dad. Nope – nothing left in the closet, or in any drawers. We searched through the few boxes and in between papers, books – nothing. Meanwhile, I still had the vile handgun case in my car that needed to be delivered to the police. The negativity of it's existence plagued me.

During the holidays we made a return trip up to Michigan and Bill's home – Joey's last home – where we too recently packed away his things. The week before traveling to Michigan, I kept getting 'nudges' to look for a set of keys – the ones Joey had mentioned in the reading and I felt certain they were somewhere in Bill's house. Once there, without much effort, I found them in a cabinet composed of many little drawers – hidden away in the back. But no passport. We still couldn't find Joey's precious passport.

Joey's set of house keys included two smaller keys that looked like they belonged to a safe or something similar. Then it occurred to me these were probably what came with the gun case – the only safe-like thing Joey possessed. Returning home, I felt compelled to try the keys on the case so I could give all of it to the police the next week. Click – the case opened! There before me was the shiny new hand gun – and resting on top of the never-used gun? Joey's passport.

More than once, a medium has stated that Spirit doesn't waste a second of communication – everything has meaning, even if we limited humans can't figure it out. Often it is truly a matter of time before the message is understood, because it relates to an occurrence that hasn't happened yet. Sometimes it's simply about remaining open to the possibility – sitting with a question, and allowing the meaning to be made clear.

Joey laid it all out as best he could for us in that first reading. The medium relayed as best she could the images and words he gave to her – and I almost blew it, saved only by the fact that the police station was closed the day I impulsively arrived to rid myself of the offensive gun case. I shudder to think that Joey's most important personal object might have been destroyed without us ever knowing. I am grateful for what surely was an intervention on the part of a Spirit team and all the nudging that followed, leading to the keys and eventually the passport.

So, the correct response to anything that doesn't immediately make sense in a mediumship reading is to let it marinate for a while – see what comes of it – and pay attention to those nudges. You never know what treasure you might find.

The Big Ask

Trust is a subject placed in my mind too many times of late to ignore. I give easy lip service to it, but what does it really mean to completely trust? Trust that everything is as it "should be." That is a BIG ask. Trust your gut – your intuition. Trust the subtle messages, and signs. My human brain fights back with annoying frequency. Thinking over the past, I'm sure to have missed messages from my gut when making poor decisions or going in a seemingly wrong direction. But perhaps my perception, my recollection, is skewed. I received clarification about one notable instance recently.

On Saturday, October 1, 2016, I was attending a workshop on "mindfulness" as part of a continuing education course. I left the house that morning feeling uneasy. Will was living with me at the time and had relapsed. He was headed for another round of treatment. This was a situation repeated many times in our family over the years. By now, at age 26, Will had come to a place of personal responsibility for his illness. There would be no arguments, or ultimatums. We would simply have a conversation and plan the next step, likely a detox. He was in college classes full-time, almost done with his degree, and I was quite sure he did not want another setback. Still sleeping when I needed to leave, I planned to talk with him later in the day – not something I looked forward to, but confident we would work it out.

As the morning workshop progressed, I had an emergent feeling of peace and calm – like a warm blanket covering my whole being. This coincided nicely with the subject matter, but went well beyond that. I had an inner sense that things would be okay with Will. Everything was as it should be. My usual obsessive worry about him when he was in an unhealthy mindset was absent. I remember being pleasantly surprised by this feeling of ease.

Sometime during the day as I was attending the workshop, Will overdosed. When I first looked into his room after arriving home and saw the bed empty, I was irritated, believing he had left the house and I wouldn't get to talk with him – he was likely avoiding the inevitable conversation. Then I turned, startled to see he had fallen forward half inside his closet, slumped onto his knees, head down, unresponsive. My internal crisis management switch flipped to "on." Will's lower legs were purple from lack of blood flow and he was incredibly hard to move, so heavy, but I somehow managed to maneuver him onto his back, give him a Narcan injection and perform chest-compressions until the paramedics arrived. I performed CPR on my own son! I tried not to think, just act. But what I did hold onto was that he had come back every time from the brink! He would come back. He had to.

There was no way of knowing how long he'd been unconscious, but it was becoming clear from previous episodes that this one was different. Multiple doses of Narcan didn't touch this. Was Fentanyl involved? He was put on full life-support. His movements were reflexive, primitive, alarming. The neurologist solemnly confirmed the next day that massive brain damage had occurred from lack of oxygen. Realization turned to heartbreak. Our efforts to talk and joke with him, anxious for him to wake up from the trauma as he had done so many times before, changed to tearful resignation. Will would never breathe on his own. Never speak, never recover to be the person he was. He had been inches from death so many times and always come back healthy and whole. We were in shock – he would not make it through this one. Faced with the painful, but only, decision to let him go, knowing it would be Will's wish, we planned for his exit, which allowed for the bittersweet gift of sitting with him for a final few days, realizing the person who was "Will" was already gone. Letting go of the rest slowly, so slowly.

I have been haunted by guilt. Why did I not "sense" the overdose that Saturday? Why was I so peaceful and calm when my son's life was leaving this earth? Why as a mother did I not feel the need to jump up from that workshop and rush home because something was terribly wrong? I had done so plenty of times before and for good reason. Where was my intuition, my gut when I needed it! Or was I "sensing" exactly what I was meant to? Just maybe Will wanted me to feel that his soul was free, finally. That his spirit was at peace and he was sharing that peace with me to let me know this was supposed to happen. I am learning to trust the latter.

At the time of the overdose, Will was in a good place with his life. He was engaged in meaningful work after having struggled so very hard for years – one step forward, two back – in the face of addiction and depression. Why did this happen when it did? After considerable soul searching, here's what I've come to radically believe – the timing of Will's death occurred precisely so as to have the greatest, positive spiritual impact for himself, his family, friends, and all the people with similar struggles whom he would never meet. I believe his work here was complete – that in the face of a devastating illness that he had never, ever gotten ahead of for more than a few months at a stretch, Will had accomplished all he could here. He died peacefully, without any collateral damage, and by that I mean he wasn't behind the wheel of a car, he hadn't abandoned a wife, child, nor been in legal trouble, lost a job, or the respect of those around him. Consequently, he is remembered for his intellect, his sweet spirit, his helpfulness, his wise, old-soul writings which have begun to influence so many. It was his time to go. It was as good as it was going to get here.

I'm learning to trust, after serious questioning, contemplation, and prayer, that my gut that day was accurate. I didn't misread the signs. Will was preparing me for the acceptance of his passing, surrounding me with love and peace as fortification for what was to come. He has let me know this is true in recent days. He has confirmed that all is as it "should be" .... because our relationship continues.

Trust. It's a big, big ask. But also, it seems, the very best answer.

902DJO

Quite often, learning the language of Spirit feels like a continuous game of charades. If I recognize a sign and acknowledge it, I'm bound to get more signs – a feedback loop slowly establishing a reliable dialogue. I can only imagine the foot tapping on the other side, while my sons patiently wait for me to "get it." Soon after Joey passed, the reading light at my kitchen table would suddenly get bright, then dim, then bright again – a few minutes of erratic flickering, then back to a steady normal for days, or weeks at a time. I thought the bulb was about to go, or something was wrong with the outlet. However, the flickering continued, more subtle in nature, and became a pattern. If I was having a difficult (sad) day, or conversely, if I had some amazing spiritual epiphany, the light would start flickering, especially as I came physically near it. I now recognize this as Will and Joey manipulating the electricity, timed to my own experiences, validating and supporting me. Other lights have flickered. The best one may have been the porch light outside a cabin where our extended family was staying on vacation. Everyone witnessed it. Everyone agreed Will and Joey wanted to make us aware of their presence. These miraculous light demonstrations are now part of a language we share across dimensions – verified through readings with mediums.

There are also instances where I've asked for a specific sign, and Will and Joey create only one amazing version – as if they are checking it off the list. Clouds come to mind. I remarked to Will and Joey that many bereaved parents were receiving messages in clouds – faces, hearts, letters – and I was feeling a little left out. That very afternoon while walking along the lakefront, I was nudged to look up to find 4 unmistakable cloud hearts, one on top of the other, one for each of my kids, with a tiny heart inside a larger heart (my oldest daughter was pregnant at the time) representing their soon-to-be nephew. Incredible! And that was it for the cloud signs – one and done. I still have the photo saved as my phone screen background and it makes me smile every time I look at it.

License plates are a recent development. After hearing a parent speak about receiving messages through significant numbers and letters appearing at just the right time, I started paying attention to license plates. Sure enough, beyond coincidence, I frequently spot Joey's birth date, transition date, initials, and versions of his name as cars zoom past, or better yet, pull in front of me on the highway. If I feel Joey's energy with me, that is when my forehead starts to tingle, I know to pay quick attention to what I'm physically seeing and hearing, and I will undoubtedly find a message from Joey. It can be so fast and subtle that I surely miss much of what he's trying to convey, but every now and then I get it right. The other day while driving, I felt Joey's presence, looked out to see "Jayco" on the back of an RV to my right (Jay being one of Joey's nicknames), with a license plate containing both Joey's birthdate and transition date, all while passing a billboard with the word "CONNECT" in giant letters. It was perfectly choreographed. Will, however, does not seem to share the same enthusiasm for license plates, although he comes through with his initials or dates on occasion. Will reserves his communication efforts for more serious endeavors, including supporting my writing. I've been told through mediums that Joey enjoys being present for day-to-day activities, celebrations, and experimenting with signs, while Will focuses on spiritual growth. Will is likely to pop in with a message during a class session I'm taking on developing connection, a meditation, or send a sign – a red cardinal, or song lyric – to validate my progress. Just as it was here on earth, they each continue to have their own personality, sense of humor, and communication style.

A few months before I caught on to the license plate game, we received a plate in the mail for my partner's new car imprinted with the following: 902DJO. At first glance I saw the "J" for Joey, thinking that was nice. Cue the foot-tapping.

Well, I realize now, not only is there a J, there's a D and a JO – Joey's middle initial and a version of his name – plus 1990 is Will's birth year, and 1992 Joey's. All of these significant numbers and letters on one license plate randomly assigned to our own car! Once I would have chalked it up to coincidence, but not anymore. It's all about paying attention – tuning in – and giving thanks for the message. No matter how long it takes to "get it."

Free Will is a Bitch

"Free will is a bitch."

This statement was made recently by Will who, as we know, physically died in October 2016. I heard this from him three years after his passing. I didn't actually hear it, but a good evidential medium did during a "reading" gifted to me because I am a parent who has lost more than one child. Some gifts are especially bittersweet. This was my sixth reading over the course of a year after losing child number two – all conducted by different, incredible people, bringing to light a continuing conversation with my boys. I might add, that it's not necessarily advisable to have so many readings back-to-back. I happened to be chosen as a "test sitter," assisting mediums to reach a certification. Along with the privilege of helping good mediums become better, I heard from my sons more frequently.

Will made the statement during a particular reading while describing his inability to change the outcome of the car accident he saw clearly from his vantage point. The event that would kill his only brother, Joey, in September 2018, almost exactly two years after Will himself had passed. Will watched the accident unfold and could not intervene! Nor could anyone else other than those physically present who made the free will choices that day to be there at that particular moment. This is what he conveyed.

What Will could and did do, he further imparted, was be the first to meet Joey's true spirit-self as it left a body about to be obliterated by a pick-up truck hitting his tiny car head-on at 58 miles per hour. The collision liberated the engine block of Joey's car and would later be found yards away on the side of the road. Joey did not feel the impact. Instead, his last image was that of his deceased brother's face through the windshield as he left his body just in time. Joey was literally "caught" by Will as his spirit flew to safety, to familiarity in a strange, new, unexpected reality, viewing the entire scene from above, objectively, a bit confused. These are also things they both have told me. Through mediums.

Will and Joey have communicated a great deal more. Information, observations, details that no one else on earth besides me would know. For instance, how I would cut the crust off of sandwiches when Will was little. He hated the crust. Or that I recently stood at the bathroom mirror while combing rapidly accumulating hair out of my brush, blaming the stress of grief as the cause of hair loss. Blaming my sons. They see me do this. They've offered these little things through mediums as evidence for their continued existence and presence.

More from them: it was Joey's time to go. If he hadn't passed from this world in that horrific accident, he would soon. His work here was complete. This is true in Will's case too.

Their paths continue somewhere else – a dimension filled with energy and mystery and love. And as hard as it is to accept, I am slowly, very slowly, coming to know this in my heart as fact. Not just believe. Know.

If anyone had told me immediately after losing a second child, I would be writing all of the above with any sense of conviction, I would have laughed out loud – how could any of this communication – this continuation – be remotely possible?

But then everything changed. I was determined to find them, having a sincere belief and early signs they were not truly "gone." In the beginning, I knew absolutely nothing about evidential mediumship. That very first family session attended by daughters/sisters Katie, Maggie, and myself, with a solidly accurate, empathic medium, upended our entire idea of the universe and all that's in it. Life changed.

I'm still wrestling with the implications of that change.

So back to the question of free will. Does it exist? Does it exist to the point where everything is random? Can it co-exist within a "soul planned" framework, or outline? There is so much more for me to learn. Sometimes my head spins. Sometimes, however, free will most certainly is a bitch.

&
....

At the age of 60, I got a tattoo, having appreciated much of this body art on others, but never having any desire to participate. Until Will died – then I understood the appeal. Here was a way to permanently inscribe my very skin with imagery in defiance of what had been taken. A way to create something physical in the aftermath, bound to last as long as I do.

This first tattoo, in memory of Will, was a collective idea, the girls and I. At the time, Joey wanted to do his own thing for Will. Turns out, he left us before he had the chance. The symbol we chose for Will is an ancient rune that means "where there's a will, there's a way" – a perfect sentiment. It's small and geometrical, with two X's stacked, one on the other. After Joey's passing, I imagined amending the original Will tattoo to represent both the boys by adding their initials, for example. I played around with a number of drawings. Nothing was satisfying.

At some point, out of the blue, the "&" symbol came to mind. The duality of Joey's life and the way in which he passed summed up, concentrated into this simple design. I made a list: youngest & oldest; brilliant & childlike; generous & self-destructive; elated & depressed; boy & man; funny & serious; expansive & stuck; before & after; wedding & wake;

best day & worst day; here & not here; tragedy & awakening. It goes on & on.

I never looked back on the decision to get the "&," putting myself on a waitlist with the artist who gave us our first tattoos. This time it would just be me with the "&" to be placed on my left wrist in honor of Joey, the mirror-imaged-spot where Will's tattoo appears on the right. Months passed and I'd all but forgotten my outreach when an email arrived saying the artist had an opening on September 1st, that's 9/1 – the date Joey left us. Without knowing, he scheduled me on the second anniversary of Joey's passing, and not only that, but his email came through at 11:11 – which I've come to learn is a sure spiritual nod, sequences of the number one being the highest angelic number – synchronicities.

The tattoo artist remembered me. He remembered the three of us almost 4 years hence, neophytes to the tattoo business, crying when we explained the reason for our group tattoo. He was gentle, kind and incredulous when I revealed why I had come for a second visit. He was also in awe of the synchronicities around the date and timing of the appointment, very much a believer in such things.

Getting down to business, he transferred the pattern, the "&," onto my skin for approval, placed so it appeared upside down in my view. I had not considered this. I had never looked at the symbol upside down, but it made sense. The person "reading" the tattoo was to see it right-side up, not me. After a moment, I adjusted to the upside-down logic and he began.

Soon it was done, disinfected, sealed up in a transparent bandage and I was on my way with grateful tears and a melancholy vow to never return. Driving home in slow, rush-hour traffic, I glanced down often to admire the upside down "&," the intense black, clean lines of permanent ink under skin, so mysterious and wonderful, thinking of Joey. Did he approve?

Then the realization. My view of the "&" symbol on its head is Joey's initials – J. D., Joseph David, the J swooping up into the D. I see my son's initials whenever I look at my wrist – it's unmistakable!

Joey knew exactly how this would play out on the anniversary of his passing – he planned it all! Joey, the giver of gifts. I imagined his delight when I finally saw the initials, felt his Joey smile take over the energy all around me – reminder that joy can be found, even on a day born of sorrow.

There's another one for the list – sorrow & joy.

Life.
Clever, clever boy.
I love you so very much Joseph David, & always will.

Taking Stock

I started keeping a notebook when it became evident we were receiving signs from Will and Joey. As I write this, there are three and a half years of almost daily entries and it's overwhelming to read through the whole thing. I am awestruck by the sheer number of communications from my sons and probably others on our Spirit support team.

Signs are incredibly personal even though the categories are general and well known – rainbows, butterflies, birds, hearts, coins, feathers, etc… the list is long. Signs from Spirit are difficult to explain because the significance, the *wow* element, is an emotional recognition often tied to something ordinary. How can you convey that? How can you bring to life the miracle out of context? That's why I tend not to try unless the encounter is so over-the-top, anyone can appreciate it. I've described a few of these in other sections of this book.

With that as a framework, and after reading through the entire *sign* notebook for the first time, I'm compelled to share the evidence of my sons' persistence in making sure we are aware they are still very much right here.

RAINBOWS

From day one, rainbows have shown up in the most unusual forms with divine timing, beginning with the spectacular display on the day of Joey's transition and Katie's wedding. Katie in particular would find rainbows everywhere during the first tender months, as if the boys were going into overdrive to get the conversation started. Rainbows appeared in drawings, store signs, bumper stickers, t-shirts, and in actual rainbow fashion, such as the one forming right in front of us over Elk Lake as we rounded the corner on our first trip back after Joey's passing. During our initial mediumship reading, the one that changed everything, the medium said, "Will and Joey are singing the song 'Rainbow Connection' with Kermit the Frog. Does that mean anything to you?" Well, yes – absolutely!

BIRDS, ETC.

Hundreds of birds, specifically blue jays for Joey and cardinals for Will, have consistently shown up. Sure they are quite common, especially if you feed them well in your backyard, but the timing of their often joint appearance has been a great validation. I know it may be hard for the person reading this to find meaning in such events, and I often hold the same skepticism about other people's myriad bird/butterfly/animal signs, but some incidents are otherwise hard to explain.

Here's an over-the-top bird sign example – the magical arrival of a Baltimore Oriole upon request. I was lamenting the fact that none had ever visited our feeder, even though neighbors reported a few Spring sitings. Orioles are unusual to spot here, but I really hoped one would drop by and asked the boys to help out. The very next day there he was! Bright orange and black, standing on the deck railing as I watched in great surprise from inside. Then, quite unexpectedly, the bird flew to the window ledge right in front of where I was standing and tapped the window – not once but twice. He immediately flew to the other side of the house and tried the living room window – tap, tap – as if wanting to be let in! Not your typical bird behavior by a not-typical bird and that's when you know. You just know.

A similar, astounding encounter occurred when I learned of the passing of a dear friend's husband – a young man who fought bravely to survive brain cancer. As I absorbed the sad news, a tiny wren tapped the window near me three times. Again, very odd bird behavior, but not only that, my friend's unusual middle name is Wren – Lily Wren. I shared this undeniable sign with her and it was a comfort to realize her husband was already reaching out – or perhaps the Hejna boys were reaching out on his behalf. Regardless, Greg has proven to be an expert communicator and Lily has her own ongoing list of remarkable signs.

Okay – one more bird episode. My daughter, Katie, has a friend who is quite open minded and spiritually inclined. One afternoon, while walking through the dunes and talking to my daughter about this friend's new tattoo, I spied two Eastern bluebirds in the tree just above me – an extremely rare occurrence in this part of the Midwest. Just as I describe the miracle of seeing the blue birds to my daughter over the phone, she texts me a photo of her psychic friend's new tattoo – two tiny, blue birds framed by a heart.

There was the case of the spectacular, giant swallowtail butterfly, never seen before or since, that followed me, circling around me as I walked up the street, within days after having a medium mention that Will and Joey would be sending a butterfly – one that I could not miss.

Deer frequent the woods around us and we see them fairly often from our window, or while walking through the dunes. But it was without fail that a complete family of deer – mom, dad with antlers, and two fawns – would show up every time my creative partner, Susan, would call or visit during the year we were most involved in putting this book together – every time, like clockwork! We could count on it – our *deer cheer squad.*

SONGS

The first undeniable song-sign was really the best and there have been hundreds – song titles, lyrics, just at the right moment – randomly playing on Google, or any other platform.

A few months after our first mediumship reading, my daughters and I decided to try a group event featuring the same medium. There would be no more than 50 attendees. It was a lot less expensive compared to an individual reading and we were anxiously hopeful the boys would come through. On the drive to the venue, I was begging Will and Joey, pleading with them to show up, the sadness of missing them was heavy. Suddenly, an unfamiliar song came on the radio – every word could have been written by them for that exact moment in time – the refrain, "... and I wish I could be there tonight," cut through my anguish with such clarity. I knew right then they would *not* be coming through that evening in the group reading. It wasn't our turn. Others in the room needed to hear from their loved ones more than we did. Consequently, I was able to let go of the expectation and enjoy an evening full of undeniably meaningful validations for grieving people, filling our hearts too and adding even more credibility to our first reading with this amazing medium. That one song opened the door to another pathway – adding to our cosmic vocabulary ... and that perfect song will show up still – just when I need it the most.

ORBS

Okay – stay with me here. When I first discovered the phenomena of capturing orbs in photographs, spheres of light from no known light source, I was quite skeptical. Sometimes these subtle balls of light come in beautiful colors and even have faces in them. I encourage anyone to explore the work of Nancy Myers (<u>theorbconnection.com</u>) to learn more about this intriguing Spirit energy. Orbs are very different from sunspots, reflections, and other light effects which is why it's important to control for all these factors. After watching her presentation, reading her book, and using her techniques – basic digital camera with a flash at night away from any artificial light – I set out to see what I could find. Theory is that Spirit energy can become briefly visible through the light of the camera flash. Very rarely, people have seen orbs with the naked eye and Nancy is one of them. In any case, I asked the Hejna boys to cooperate as I brought the camera out at a family gathering with all their favorite people and Joey's dog in attendance, figuring the boys would surely be floating about. I took plenty of shots – inside, outside, with one person, the whole group, etc. The next day I held my breath while sifting carefully through the images – looking for any sign of an orb. Nothing. Nothing! Oh well – so much for that, I thought. Disappointed, I stowed the camera.

But soon after, I got a *nudge* to look at the photos again – to put them up on a larger screen and really look. Well – how could I have missed them? There were dozens! Some in between family members gathered for dinner outside and many more floating in the tall trees, like a huge Spirit contingent in attendance. The orbs appeared more subtle and smaller than I expected, but unmistakable! The Hejna boys did not disappoint after all and they brought a crowd. As is usually the case, it took a good nudge and some time for me to catch on.

Occasionally I'll bring my camera out during meaningful events to capture what I can, however, the most amazing orb experience happened in real time during an online, Zoom session where I was participating in an experiment with a specific form of spiritual connection. Before the interview, I was testing out my iPad camera, having flipped it around to view me against a black background and WHOOSH, right above and behind my head, a small, white orb traveled quickly past as I watched it on the screen! I was speechless. What a beautiful gift from the usually unseen world.

LOVELY TOKENS
I have a basket full of heart shaped rocks, and numerous collected feathers – precious gifts. The little kitchen light next to my favorite photo of Will and Joey continues to flicker most days – just like a brief 'hello' – "The boys are

here!," I'll announce when I see it, with a smile and happy heart. I expect my *sign* notebook will contain many new and miraculous entries the next time I read through in astonishment – in deep gratitude – for the essential love that fuels our ongoing cosmic conversation.

Bread Crumbs

The first of a long list of books I consumed to learn about the afterlife was *Soul Shift,* by Mark Ireland. I was drawn to his book because Mark is a parent who lost a child and also happens to be the son of the famous medium, Richard Ireland. *Soul Shift* details Mark's awakening to his own latent mediumistic abilities which opened the door to communication with his son in Spirit, Brandon. Mark had limited interest in his famous father's career and celebrity, but always respected the work. Brandon's passing shattered his perspective and launched Mark into new directions, eventually leading to the creation, along with the lovely Elizabeth Boisson, of Helping Parents Heal – a support network for bereaved parents. What began as a few local chapters centered in the Western US has now grown internationally with a membership of over 20,000 parents receiving online and in-person support across the globe. Members are referred to as 'shining light parents' and the overall philosophy of the group is hopeful – joy can be found even after the most devastating of losses. Relationships with our loved ones in Spirit continue and helping others is the best way to heal. It is an open minded, non-dogmatic group with the ability to help transform grief into peace. I belong to this organization and it has made a tremendous difference. These are my people – possibly the only ones who can truly understand. I cannot recommend

Helping Parents Heal highly enough to anyone navigating this difficult path (helpingparentsheal.org).

Another project that was sparked by Mark's son's passing was the certification of evidential mediums. It is crucial to trust that a mediumistic reading is valid, the medium is compassionate and capable, and in the business for the right reasons – to serve others. Being subjected to a poor or fraudulent reading can be devastating to anyone, especially a grieving parent so Mark created a process to certify mediums whereby at least five different 'test sitters' under controlled, double-blind conditions, rate the veracity of the medium's statements. The transcribed sessions are scored and, if the medium passes, they are listed on his website findacertifiedmedium.com. Mark does not charge fees for the certification and listing process.

I've had the great privilege of 'sitting' for his program as a volunteer, affording me wonderful connections with my sons and others. My mother-in-law, who passed several years ago, is a frequent spiritual attendee during test readings. She shows up with a fabulous sense of humor, quirky bits of evidence, and has said (through mediums) that she really enjoys being part of the process. Once, as she was signing-off during a session, she exclaimed, "goodbye now – I'm off to feed the ducks," knowing this would bring a smile to my face, remembering all the times she took my children, her grandchildren, to the harbor on Lake Michigan, bags of old bread and crackers in hand, to feed the ducks. In other readings she has joked about her fad diets, her tendency in life to collect way too many things, the cheesy potato casseroles she would cook for a crowd, and her love of entertaining in her beautiful Victorian home – amazing pieces of evidence. My sons have made it clear they willingly participate in the certification readings as part of our work together – to bring hope to others via the practice of evidential mediumship. If Will and Joey participate in full force during a reading, I'm confident the medium involved has met their approval. If, on the other hand, the boys are quiet, or make a statement like, "there's a time and place for everything," instead of bringing more of themselves to the session, I'll know the medium isn't likely ready for prime time.

Mollie Morningstar, the first medium my daughters and I sat with in Chicago, who gave the reading that changed our lives, happens to be good friends with Mark Ireland and his wife. I mentioned Mark's book during our session and Mollie was delighted, encouraging our budding involvement in Helping Parents Heal. Months later, after getting to know Mark, he relayed astounding messages Mollie has relayed from their son Brandon which Mark's included in his own writings, however I knew none of this when we scheduled our initial session with Mollie. My daughter chose Mollie quite by chance, or so it seemed.

I picked *Soul Shift* from a sea of books quite *randomly*, which led me to Helping Parents Heal – a family of amazing people and resources shaping the work I feel called to do with my sons, including certify good mediums and support grieving parents. Meanwhile my daughter *randomly* chose Mollie for our first life-changing reading who *happens* to be friends with Mark who then validated Mollie's fine work with his own evidence, furthering our confidence that she's the real deal. Looking back, I would say the word *orchestrated* is a more accurate descriptor for how these events have unfolded.

I'm learning that if my heart is on the right path, things line-up as if by magic – the perfect person, book, phone call, class, etc. appears just at the perfect moment. Bread crumbs in the form of little intuitive nudges are there if I'm able to trust them. Sometimes I can sense this divine direction in real time, but more often it's through hindsight.

And you can bet I ask for help, loud and clear, when faced with a tough situation, knowing a very trustworthy and loving Spirit team will shine a light – illuminating the best way forward.

All I have to do is follow.

Ready

It won't be easy.

Etching the diamond facade calls
for a tool of exquisite sharpness, a steady hand.

The word "open" to be inscribed carefully, winding
between keepsakes
left there, now imbedded.

Offerings from those who circled just close enough
to imagine what might have been.

Dust settled, loss layers silenced, there is
work to be done.

It's possible once again to enter the portal through the
mother heart,
into the light,
into the love,
beyond place,
beyond all time.

Perfect

I am newly a grandmother and highly recommend it. There is nothing, nothing, like new baby energy to fill up the heart and soul. I had the extreme privilege, thanks to my lovely daughter, Katie, and son-in-law, Adam, to be present when this baby was born. I met him immediately after the cord was cut, hollering and slick, all muscles and fuzzy copper hair. He came out fully cooked! It feels to my mother-meets-grandmother-heart like he is all four of my own babies rolled up into one juicy bundle of love.

Maggie, now Aunt Maggie, was also at the birth. As the new baby was being tended to, cleaned up, weighed, we both, Maggie and I, took pains to look very, very closely at his ears, exchanging secretive glances. Huh. They looked fine? He was pronounced perfect by the clinicians. Maybe that part of the reading was wrong, we thought. Relief.

About six months before the birth, I received a reading from a talented medium, who accurately predicted this baby would be born a healthy boy. The medium connected extremely well to Joey. I had had other excellent readings by this time, and was familiar with Joey's way of communicating. It happened to be a "test reading" to help the medium earn "certified" status, a process I participated in as a "test sitter" off-and-on throughout the year. Each reading with a different medium was a very controlled, double-blind situation, meaning both the medium and myself were unknown to the other. Joey seemed intent on assisting the medium this day by providing wonderful details and it was a phenomenal session. Toward the end, the medium was hesitant to pass along a piece of information, but Joey was insistent. He conveyed that Katie's baby would have something, "....very, very, very minor wrong with his right ear," the medium said. "I'm not sure what it is exactly, but it's not going to be big deal and this is how you'll know that Joey is with the baby and knows all about him." I shared this particular detail with only a few people, Maggie being one, and certainly did not share it with the mom-to-be. How could we be sure anyway? The medium could be wrong and no one needed unnecessary worry.

Day two in the maternity wing with baby and mama coming along beautifully. The rest of the usual testing being completed – eyes, ears, etc. "We are going to have to repeat the hearing test tomorrow," the nurse stated. "It may just be some fluid in his right ear. We couldn't' get a clear test today." Katie told me this over the phone when I called to check in. My heart skipped several beats. The reading was spot on! Joey had been involved in this baby's development all along! The evidence could not have come from anyone here. Anyone physically here. However, this sense of elation was mixed with concern that something was wrong with the baby's ear. Katie was rightly anxious. The nurse had implied the problem was probably temporary, but as a worried new mother, it didn't help. So I told her. I told Katie what the medium had predicted. That Joey knew this would happen and he also guaranteed it to be, "very, very, very minor." The baby would be absolutely fine. Katie wasn't sure how to take it all in and I regret this was definitely too much information at the time, shared only because I wanted to ease her mind – and for goodness sake it seemed too good! Just too good – the evidence.

Day three in the maternity wing with preparations to go home in progress, the nurse announced the baby had passed his follow-up hearing test with flying colors! His right ear was fine – the loss temporary. "It must have been residual fluid," the nurse stated. We looked at each other, stunned, relieved, with the implications of Joey's very accurate "sign" sinking in. He's still right here, we silently concluded. There can be no doubt. What other explanation is there?

Will and Joe are both still right here, regularly looking in on their little nephew. At times when the baby is staring excitedly at the ceiling, I imagine his spirit uncles are painting rainbows in the air, visible only to his clear, new-baby eyes. And most certainly whispering "I love you" into tiny perfect ears.

Plans

Long after their leaving, I couldn't imagine ...

What moments of this life would I choose to live again?

But now it's obvious because I rocked a baby to sleep as he whispered
my new name – Nana.

And the tears appeared, tears
of good heartache because I was reminded
of the magic night stillness so many years ago with a baby of mine,
after the nursing.

Just us –
rocking silently to the rhythm of tiny breath
perfect weight in my arms.

I will pick one night for each of the four, returning
somewhere mid-infancy and spend
one fourth of eternity, whatever that might be,
one after the other,
rocking in the quiet,
with a heart full to bursting.

Acknowledgements

As are all creative efforts, I believe, this book has been a collaborative process unfolding in multiple dimensions. There is absolutely no question that minds vastly more intelligent and capable than my own have been involved – seen and unseen.

On the earth-side book designer, Susan Kenn, my creative friend and partner with a beautiful vision, has most directly helped to bring *Rainbow Hair* to life. It is no coincidence that every time we discussed the book's progress, Susan would have the perfect suggestion at hand to set the course, leading to a burst of creative energy. I am beyond grateful for Susan's ability to see the forest, and not just the trees – always encouraging – always believing in the message. Thank you.

Reading raw content for the benefit of the writer is a daunting task, especially if the emotional triggers can be hard to navigate. In the case of this book, early readers had to be the same people most affected by events – to validate the honesty of the telling and help fill any gaps. Katie and Maggie Hejna, daughters from this lifetime and probably many others, provided invaluable feedback. I know it was not easy to read – to re-live things. This is also true for son-in-law, Adam Selkirk, and my partner in life, Mauro Crestani, jumping back into difficult territory without hesitation.

Jennifer Taylor Henderson, dearest friend and emotional touch stone, thoughtfully read, cried, rejoiced and made diligent notes in the margins. I thank you all for your time, comments, and blessings to go forward.

If Jennifer is the friend holding one of my hands, Dalia Lietuvninkas is holding the other. She has been a source of strength for many years and was the first one to hug me fiercely on that fateful wedding day and whisper in my ear, "They are together. Your boys are together. I know it. I know it." Dodi Krug created the three beautiful bracelets described in *The Reading*. She doesn't mind in the least that Will and Joey were watching over her shoulder with plans to use her future gift as a fabulous validation of their presence. Thank you Dodi for your generosity. To ex-husband, Bill, and the extended Hejna family, both here and across the veil, deep gratitude for your endless support and acceptance. To all the friends who donated the trees, the ones who have cried with us, and the ones who aren't afraid to ask, "How are you doing?" – or, better yet, "Have you heard from the boys lately?"

Not coincidently, writer/editor, Michael Kimball, came into the process at just the right moment, after our original editor dropped out due to time constraints, suggesting his colleague Michael might be a good fit. He was perfect. Michael's thorough editorial suggestions and encouraging words gave Susan and I the exhilarating push to pursue publishing. He embraced the content with an excitement for what the manuscript might become, and his summary email to me contained some of the sweetest words I've ever read: "Whatever you decide to do with it, you should do it with confidence. You've already made something wonderful." Thank you Michael.

I would also like to thank my (step)grandson, Elliott, for lending his rainbow hair collage that so perfectly represents the essence of the book, and for the honest, four-year-old recounting of the vision which was the beginning of it all. Thank you Elliott.

Thank you to Elizabeth Boisson for her tireless work on behalf of every 'shining light' parent, and who has astonishingly also become a friend. Your beautiful 'Foreword' to this book has captured it gorgeously and set it afire. Lisa Hagan has been a source of encouragement and wisdom throughout the publishing process. Thank you, Lisa, for your steadfast belief in what we could do together.

Our path is forever changed by the sessions with gifted evidential mediums, Mollie Morningstar, Rachel Pearson, Daniel John, Lisa Wilcoxson, and Manisha Akhauri, who collectively provided direct evidence that the boys are truly still right here! The hope is real and I thank you from the bottom of my heart.

As for the unseen inspirers, my sons lead the pack. Will and Joey have been behind, under, over, and through this project from the beginning. In almost every mediumship reading, they've emphatically encouraged the writing, made clear the purpose of helping others, and shown they are always working with me. My mother has also given her extra-dimensional blessing: "Don't hold back. Tell the truth. Don't worry about me." She undoubtedly knew I was concerned about hurting her feelings. Thank you, Mom, for your strength and guidance.

I send deep, deep gratitude to all who've made *Rainbow Hair* possible. May this wonderful collaboration bring healing and peace to those in need.

Appendix

Resources

The organization, *Helping Parents Heal* (helpingparentsheal.org), tops my list of critically important resources. I believe that anyone who has had a child pass could benefit from the wealth of information which includes names of providers, books, and recordings of online presentations via YouTube. There are frequent supportive meetings, both virtual and in-person, and smaller groups available specifically for grieving fathers, siblings, loss due to suicide, and many more.

MEDIUMS

Below are people with whom I've had personal experience and highly recommend. Other excellent evidential mediums can be found at helpingparentsheal.org (listed under 'providers') and findacertifiedmedium.com.

- Mollie Morningstar molliemorningstar.com
- Rachel Pearson rachelpearson.net
- Daniel John danieljohnmedium.com
- Lisa Wilcoxson phoenixmedium.com
- Manisha Akhauri Abundant Soul Connections (Facebook) abundantsoulconnections@gmail.com

BOOKS

Out of all that I've read, these are the ones I return to again and again.

- Soul Shift, by Mark Ireland
- Walking in the Garden of Souls, by George Anderson
- Still Right Here, by Suzanne Giesemann
- Wolf's Message, by Suzanne Giesemann
- Proof of Heaven, by Eben Alexander
- Destiny of Souls, by Michael Newton
- Signs, by Laura Lynne Jackson
- Hello from Heaven, by Bill & Judy Guggenheim
- Finding Meaning, by David Kessler
- Permission to Mourn, by Tom Zuba
- Life to Afterlife, Helping Parents Heal – the Book, compiled by Elizabeth Boisson
- My Search for Christopher on the Other Side, by Joe McQuillen
- Gathering at the Doorway, compiled by Camille Dan
- The Afterlife Frequency, by Mark Anthony

WHAT PEOPLE ARE SAYING ABOUT RAINBOW HAIR

"I loved Nancy's book *Rainbow Hair*. The heartbreaking story of losing her boys Will and Joey only to rediscover them in spirit. Letting us know that not only are they accessible in spirit but they are healed and happy.

And although it's quite evident that Nancy's heart will remain broken until reunited with her sons on the other side, she remains here. Two feet on the ground. A loving mother and grandmother.

Nancy's book follows no timeline and like the other side it's not linear. It bounces from a description to a poem, to a revelation, and then back again. And that makes it her story and that makes it perfect. It's an important book for any grieving parent who question's if they are doing it right.

Because like Nancy's book, no matter where you are in the process, it's where you ought to be. And like Nancy's book. That's perfect."

–**Joe McQuillen**, speaker and author of *My Search for Christopher on the Other Side* and *We're Not Done Yet, Pop*

"*Rainbow Hair* is an incredibly tragic, yet powerful and beautiful story, of resilience, hope, and everlasting love. Nancy inspires those of us who have lost a child to reexamine our connections with our children in spirit. Although we continue to mourn the loss of their physical presence, in time, we learn to develop an even deeper relationship with our children who have left their physical beings. Their love, their energy, are everlasting. The signs are present and undeniable, if we chose to be open to them. Grieving is a necessary process, and not a linear one. The deep pangs of longing will come and go, but by remaining focused and committing to seek the light, we will find joy and a renewed and powerful connection to our children who have transitioned to the other side of the veil. Nancy's words profoundly resonated with me but did so in a visceral sense when she discovered her eldest son, as my experience was eerily similar. Nancy Hejna's *Rainbow Hair* is a must read for all who are navigating this journey of life after the loss of a child, and in her case, not one, but two sons: two years apart, at the same time of year, and at the same ages. Nancy is indeed a "shining light parent," but she is also a courageous warrior, overcoming the invisible scars from a battle that is seemingly insurmountable."

–**Margaret Thompson**, author of *Finding Color in the Darkness: Losing My Son to Bipolar Disorder*

"*Rainbow Hair* by Nancy Hejna is a compelling and touching story. I can't imagine the loss of two sons in the span of two years. I know the pain of that loss, for I have lost a son, as well. Nancy's writing touches my soul, and I admire her strength."

–**Mark Petruzzi**, author of, *Rockets in the Sky: One Man's journey of healing the loss of a child.*

About the Author

Nancy is a retired pediatric occupational therapist, residing in the Miller neighborhood of Gary, Indiana, at the southernmost point of Lake Michigan. Primarily a visual artist, she has harbored a secret wish to write and has done so with some urgency over the past few years. She enjoys walking the Indiana dunes with partner, Mauro, and spending time with her beautiful children, grandchildren, beloved cats, and backyard chickens. www. nancyhejna.com

Made in the USA
Monee, IL
14 September 2023